The
Constant Contact
Guide to
Email
Marketing

Constant Contact®

The
Constant Contact
Guide to
Email Marketing

ERIC GROVES

WILEY

John Wiley & Sons, Inc.

Library of Congress Cataloging-in-Publication Data:

The Constant Contact guide to email marketing/Constant Contact, Inc.
   p. cm.
  ISBN 978-0-470-50341-6 (cloth)
  1. Internet marketing.   2. Electronic mail systems.   I. Constant Contact, Inc.
II. Title: Guide to email marketing.
HF5415.1265.C658 2009
658.8'72–dc22

                                                                    2009021637

Printed in the United States of America.
10 9 8 7 6 5 4 3 2

Contents

Contents

Acknowledgements

At Constant Contact it always starts and finishes with our customers, without whom I would have very little to write about. To all of those customers who have shared with me and my colleagues at Constant Contact their knowledge and experiences, I extend my most grateful thanks.

A special thank you to John Wiley & Sons, Inc., Senior Editor Richard Narramore, who quickly caught onto Constant Contact's passion to educate small businesses and organizations on the power of email marketing and supported us endlessly in our pursuit to bring this book to market. Thanks to the other members of our team at Wiley: Ann Kenny and Kate Lindsay. They helped me navigate the steps as a first-time author.

To Matt Wagner of Fresh Books Literary Agency for guiding us through this great opportunity and working tirelessly to bring this book to fruition.

To the people of Constant Contact, who strive every day to revolutionize the success formula for small businesses and organizations, a piece of what I have learned from all of you is embedded within every page of this book. To Gail Goodman, Bob Nault, Tom Howd, Ellen Brezniak, Bob Nicoson, John Walsh, Steve Wasserman, Dan Richards, and Nancie Freitas, thanks for your leadership. And to the entire Constant Contact Global Market Development Team, a special thanks for the inspiration you provide me on a daily basis.

A special word of thanks to John Arnold for coaching me through the process, expanding my words, assembling the pieces, and driving this project to completion.

Thanks also to Constant Contact's partners, including SCORE, SBDCs, and Chambers of Commerce, that support us in our mission to educate every small business or organization that wants to understand the Power of Relationships.

And last, to my wife Tracy and my children Madeline and Mitchell for all of their support and encouragement as I toiled away in the office writing this book.

The 40 "Know It or Blow It" Rules of Email Marketing

Email marketing is an amazingly cost-effective way to build relationships that drive business success. In today's challenging economic times, this cost advantage makes email marketing arguably the most powerful tool for building any business.

But the main advantage of email marketing is not cost. Email is simply the most effective way to stay in touch with most of your customers. If you're like many businesses, the 2009 recession forced you to hunker down and focus on driving business and sales from those most likely to buy—people you already have a relationship with—and that's what email marketing is all about.

Email marketing is powerful, but it's also a challenge because the inbox is a hostile environment. Whether your email is noteworthy or not-worthy depends on your ability to stick to the fundamentals of authentic relationship building with your customers. That's what this book is about—how to use email to build long-lasting customer relationships.

Over the years, we at Constant Contact have made it our mission to collect, create, refine, and share email marketing best practices with our customers. We're proud to now share these with you in this book—strategies that have contributed to the success of hundreds of thousands of businesses around the globe. On a daily basis we interact with thousands of business owners and non-profits just like you on the phone, online via webinars, and in person at live seminars held throughout the United States. These interactions provide us with regular feedback and fascinating lessons on the rapidly evolving world of email marketing.

Here are some examples of small businesses and non-profits who have discovered a broad range of benefits of email marketing:

> *"We track all of our participants and have found that more than 53% of them found out about us through the Internet or our email newsletter. Email marketing is only a fraction of the cost of print ads and it brings in a phenomenal ROI."*
> **—Girls Learn to Ride**

> *"I can't believe the number of people who walk into our restaurants and redeem coupons. Before I tried email marketing, I would put a coupon in the local newspaper—but fewer than 10 people would redeem it. I then put the same coupon in an email and sent it to 400 people. I saw 100 email coupons redeemed that month!"*
> **—Fajita Grill**

> *"For our 35th anniversary, we sent a 'save the date' email to 3,000 people. At 42 cents a stamp, that would be over $1,000 worth of postage we've saved from just one mailing."*
> **—Women Employed**

> *"Most of all, email marketing has helped us stay connected, build community, and inspire people."*
> **—Episcopal Diocese of Atlanta**

> *"Our revenue from return customers has increased about 30% since we began sending out our 'New Arrivals' email campaign. We've found that a number of customers who have never purchased from us before will buy after we send out an email campaign."*
> **—Bijoux Mart International**

I know the email strategies in this book work because I have personally taught them to thousands of small business owners and watched the results. Constant Contact's success is directly attributable to the fact that we have helped so many of them grow their organizations. In addition, I used these same email strategies to help build Constant Contact from an unknown technology startup into an industry-leading public company. When I arrived in 2001, we had

10 customers and roughly $100 a month in revenue. Now, we are the largest provider of email marketing services for small- to medium-sized businesses, with 300,000 customers in 120 countries and 500+ employees. I hope you'll find a path to greater business success in the pages that follow.

Since this book is for busy leaders who don't have a lot of time, I've decided to use Chapter 1 to summarize all the email marketing success fundamentals contained in this book, so you can quickly decide which of your own email practices need immediate attention.

The rest of the book will help you build a comprehensive email marketing strategy for your business.

Ten Keys to Your Overall Email Marketing Success

If you learn nothing else from this book, I recommend you master the following ten principles. Most of the statistics that suggest high returns on email marketing investment depend on how closely you adhere to these basics.

1. **Only send email to people who know you.** People open email from people they know, and they delete email from people they don't recognize or mark it as spam. It doesn't even matter what's legal or ethical. If your business makes a habit of emailing total strangers, then your reputation, your budget, and your growth will suffer for it. You can read about building a good email list in Chapter 5.

2. **Don't treat email addresses like email addresses; treat them like relationships.** An email address is one of the most personal things someone can share with your business because it's an invitation to send your messages to a place where he or she sends and receives personal communications as well as business ones. Email doesn't work if it feels like a computer-generated HTML document. It has to come across as being part of a meaningful relationship. You can read about building relationships in Chapter 2.

3. **Send relevant content that has value to your recipient.** You probably weren't going to send irrelevant, valueless content on purpose, but content with good intentions isn't the same thing as value and relevance. In order to ensure that your emails are valuable and relevant, you have to know exactly what your audience wants. You have to be a good listener to be a good

communicator. You can find more about creating relevance and value in your content in Chapter 7.

4. **Engage your audience in the content you write.** This requires attention-grabbing subject lines, clear headlines, and thoughtful content. You can read about what makes email content engaging in Chapter 7.

5. **Maximize your delivery rate.** Getting email delivered is harder than you might think. Internet Service Providers ("ISPs") such as Yahoo!, AOL, and Hotmail work diligently to block emails from unwanted senders. If your email isn't up to professional standards in reputation, technology, or permission, you might as well be sending your email directly to the junk folder. You can read about maximizing delivery in Chapter 11.

6. **Don't share email lists with anyone.** Your email list is a valuable asset. It will lose value if you loan it to someone else because the people on your list won't recognize a foreign sender. You should never borrow an email list from someone else. That list is full of people who aren't familiar with your business, and you

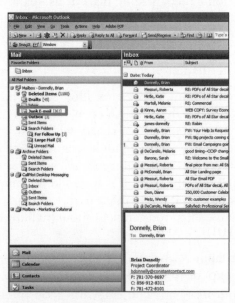

Figure 1.1   Avoiding the junk folder is one of the keys to successful email marketing.

are likely to attract more enemies than friends. You can read about protecting your email list in Chapter 6.

7. **Set expectations with your recipients.** When someone signs up to receive your email communications, they do so with the expectation of receiving something of value. If you don't communicate clearly what that value is, your audience will draw their own conclusions. Tell your audience what you'll be sending and how often you'll be sending it. That way, you'll defeat any value, relevance, and frequency objections before your audience even signs up. You can read more about setting expectations in Chapter 4.

8. **Look professional whenever you communicate.** If you're a salesperson, you know how to dress for success. Similarly, if you're an email, you need to look familiar, inviting, and consistent. You can read more about creating an email with a friendly professional identity in Chapter 9.

9. **Be ready to respond.** Email communications can be highly automated, in an off-putting way that distances you from your customers. Don't set an email auto reply in your in-box and take a mental vacation. Keep an eye on your communications and your responses so you can take action, make changes, and repeat positive results. You can read more about responding to your emails in Chapter 12.

10. **Regularly review your campaign results.** The longer you practice marketing the more you realize how unpredictable your results will be if you don't analyze your past and make adjustments based on your data. Use email tracking reports to help you improve, progress, and grow. You can read about email tracking reports in Chapter 12.

Ten Things Your Customers Expect You to Do

Most marketing failures happen because the business worries more about what to expect from its customers than what its customers expect from the company. The problem is, it's not easy to know exactly what your customers expect. You have to ask them constantly, and you have to believe them, which is even harder than asking. Here's what

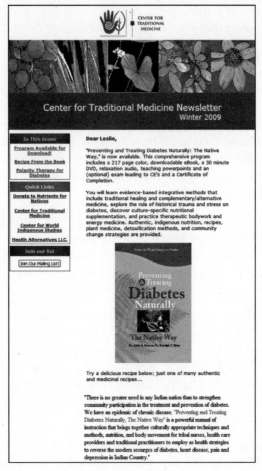

Figure 1.2   Professional looking emails reinforce your brand and identity.

Constant Contact has learned about meeting customer expectations when it comes to email marketing. Your customers expect you to:

1. **Protect them.** Storing data in a secure environment is critical, but that's not all there is to privacy. You need a privacy policy, and you need to be sensitive to the amount of intrusion you cause your customers. You can read more about privacy in Chapter 4.

2. **Know them.** Your customers don't lack information, they lack *personalized* relevant information. You don't need to know every detail about your customers, but you have to make them

Figure 1.3   Give your subscribers a link to your privacy policy.

feel like you know them so you can target your communications
to their interests. You can find out how to determine what your
customers want you to know about them in Chapter 5.

3. **Help them.** Email is noise when it doesn't solve a problem or
leave the recipient better off than she was before reading the
email. To be successful at email marketing, your emails have
to help save time, money, and angst. You can read more about
helpful email content in Chapter 7.

4. **Promise them.** Your business makes promises, regardless of
whether you intend to. When you send out a message that
describes your products or services, someone has to believe it in
order to buy it. When someone believes you, it's a promise you
need to keep if you want to keep that customer. When someone
subscribes to your email list, you have also made a promise to
send only what the subscriber believes he will receive. You can
read more about making promises and sending only what you
promised in Chapter 4.

5. **Respond to them.** Email is a two-way form of communication. Your audience wants you to respond when they interact with your emails. They can reply, click, block, unsubscribe, and forward your emails, and every form of response deserves an appropriate follow up from you. You can read more about responding to email interaction in Chapter 12.

6. **Teach them.** People make more educated decisions than they used to because there is so much information available. Consumers want to justify their purchase decisions with good information, and emails are perfect for delivering quality information in a concise format. You can read about creating good email content that makes your audience smarter in Chapter 7.

7. **Grab them.** Email inboxes are crowded with messages because of spam and because people subscribe to a lot of email lists. Most people don't have time to read all the emails they receive, and they want someone to help them prioritize the information in their inbox. Your emails have to grab attention and deliver your message clearly. You can read more about grabbing your audience's attention in Chapter 7.

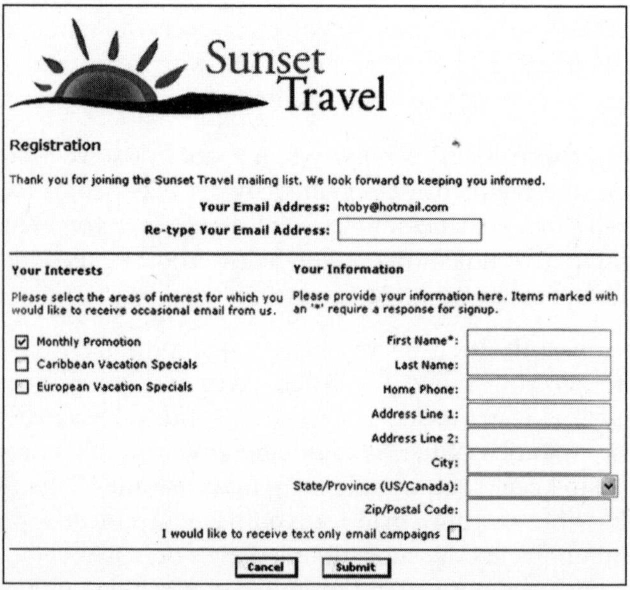

Figure 1.4   Ask your email subscribers to share their interests.

8. **Ask them.** It's just as classy to ask for your customer's permission to start periodic emailing as it is to ask your girlfriend's parents to start dating. It's old-fashioned, effective, and will probably make you look better than your competition. You can read more about asking for permission in Chapter 4.

9. **Give them options.** Your audience isn't likely to simply respond to an offer to "Join Our Email Blast." You need to give people choices so they can choose the information they want to receive and make changes when their interests shift. You can read more about providing list options in Chapter 5.

10. **Free them.** It's easy to think that your email list is too valuable to let anyone easily remove herself. Think again. You need to make it easy for someone to unsubscribe or move from one email list to another. Put an unsubscribe link in every email and let your audience remove themselves from your list permanently with one click. You can read more about allowing and minimizing unsubscribe requests in Chapter 4.

Ten Ways to Get Your Business in Trouble with Email

How could something so easy, so cost-effective, and so powerful get you in trouble? It usually happens the moment you think that easy, cost-effective, and powerful tools can't possibly be abused.

1. **Get spam complaints.** Spam is in the eye of the receiver. If your audience thinks your email is spam, all they have to do in most cases is click one button in their email program, and your email address is flagged as possible spam forever. Spam complaints destroy your deliverability and reputation. To avoid spam complaints, you have to avoid looking like spam. You can read more about spam complaints in Chapter 4.

2. **Use deceptive ways to collect contact information.** You can find email addresses everywhere you look, but not everything shiny is gold. Collecting email addresses from web sites, directories, and web-crawling computer programs will give your email list more spam complaints than sales. You can read more about proper email address collection in Chapter 4.

3. **Violate the CAN-SPAM Act.** Consumers hate spam, so Congress decided to take action on spammers by creating the CAN-SPAM Act. You can be fined if you violate the CAN-SPAM Act, but the laws also shed light on the email marketing practices that consumers dislike the most. You can read about the CAN-SPAM Act in Chapter 4.

4. **Send too much email.** Your business has to survive, and regular communications are the key to staying top of mind with customers. Sending the right amount of content at the proper frequency is a balance that will reward you if you practice keeping your finger off the "send" button when your customers aren't ready to hear from you. You can read more about over-communication in Chapter 12.

5. **Buy an email list.** Email list purchases or rentals fail not because of the quality of the list, but rather because consumers dislike receiving unfamiliar emails. You can read more about email list building in Chapter 5.

6. **Share your email list unintentionally.** Sharing your email doesn't necessarily have to involve handing a disk to a friend or colleague. When you send an email with hundreds of email addresses copied into the cc field, you are sharing your entire list with everyone you're sending to. You can read more about the proper ways to send email in Chapter 4.

7. **Share your business with a spammer.** If you send email from an email server that also hosts other businesses, that server is only as good as the reputation of the other people who send email from that server. If your shared hosting partners are spamming people, your emails can be flagged as spam by email programs. Using an email service with a good reputation is critical to your deliverability. Read more about sender reputation in Chapter 4.

8. **Go it alone.** Effective email marketing is nearly impossible without partners to help you with formatting, delivery, and strategy. Just like a good CEO surrounds herself with key people to grow a business, a good email marketer is surrounded by partners who are invested in the success of the business. You can read more about key partners in Chapter 11.

9. **Hide your identity.** Even if your audience knows you, they still have to recognize you. Your email's "from" line has to be familiar, your brand has to be prominent, and your email address has to look friendly to the companies that decide which emails to deliver and which to send to the junk folder. You can read more about creating familiar emails in Chapter 9.

10. **Fail to plan.** If you're going to invest time, energy, effort, and money in an email marketing program, take the time to plan the steps necessary to be successful. You can read more about planning for success in Chapters 2 and 3.

Ten Reasons to Use an Email Marketing Service Provider

Many small businesses use Microsoft Outlook or a similar email program when they start doing email marketing. The problem is that these applications were designed for one-to-one communications. They can work fine for sending email to a few dozen people. But using Outlook to help you send hundreds or thousands of emails to your customers is like using a speaker phone to deliver a speech in an auditorium. Email marketing can have a powerful impact on your business, and you need tools that are designed for the task. If you are serious enough about email marketing to pick up this book, you should consider using an email service like Constant Contact. (We're the largest by far, and the best [we believe!], but there are other ones out there.) Email services help you perfect your strategy, manage your data, design your emails, and track your results.

1. **Look professional.** Unless you're an HTML programmer who knows how every email program used by your customers will render your code differently, you should consider using an Email Service Provider (ESP) to help you with elements such as colors, fonts, images, and page designs.

2. **Easily conform to CAN-SPAM regulations.** All reputable email service providers build legal requirements into their platforms so you don't have to worry about compliance.

3. **Learn best practices.** Email service companies send a lot of emails. The best ones listen to their customers, study their customers' results, and share the best practices with others so

everyone can grow. Go with an email service that embraces the philosophy that when customers are successful, the company is successful.

4. **Give customers and easy way to unsubscribe.** Keeping track of the people who no longer want your emails is not only professional, it's a legal requirement. Email services include easy and safe unsubscribe links in every email that automatically remove anyone who clicks on them and keeps track of your unsubscribed customers so you can't inadvertently add them back.

5. **List management.** Sending email to a list professionally isn't as simple as cutting and pasting email addresses into a program. Email services allow you to manage your customers' personal information and preferences so your emails are customized and your subscribers are segmented into categories and interests.

6. **Track results.** If you want to see who's opening, forwarding, and clicking on your emails, you need an email service that gives you tracking reports. Email services can also tell you which

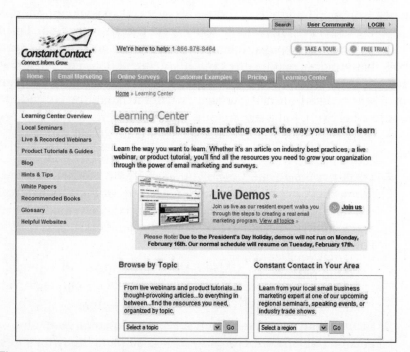

Figure 1.5   Email services share the best practices with their customers.

emails bounced, why they bounced, and which subscribers opted out of your communications.

7. **Maximize delivery to the inbox.** Your customers' Internet Service Providers want to deliver wanted email while blocking unwanted email, so they pay close attention to the reputation of the sender when they decide whether to deliver or block emails to their customers. If you use an email service that is friendly to ISPs and blocks uninvited spammers from using their services, you'll have a higher delivery rate. If you use your own email server to deliver your mail, you'll start with no reputation at all, and you'll probably experience average delivery rates.

8. **Automate where appropriate.** Email services are constantly developing new tools that help you to automate your strategy so you can spend more time with your customers. Automated features include signup forms that feed customer information into your database, auto responders that send selected emails after a specified event, and email templates that automatically lay out your content and brand elements into eye catching arrangements.

9. **Cost a fraction of a penny per communication.** Perhaps the best email marketing benefit involves the low cost of sending lots of emails to lots of people. Good email services pass these low costs on to their customers in the form of fixed monthly fees for unlimited emails or price breaks for large list holders.

10. **Provide tools that impact your profits.** Where do you turn when you need a library of stock photography, a way to archive your emails to your web site, or online surveys to help you understand your customers better? Any good Email Service Provider will offer these tools and will be constantly finding ways to make your emails come to life and give you the greatest return on your investment in their products and services.

At this point your mind is either spinning with ideas on how to put these rules into practice for your business or you are wondering how to get started. The great news is that in both cases the answers lie in reading on! You may think that sending an email marketing campaign is fairly simple and you would be right. However, email marketing is not about sending email, it's about getting people to read it! So let's get started.

2

The Power of Email Relationships

Have you ever entered a store by opening a door and heard a bell ring? That bell tells store owners that it's time to drop what they're doing and focus on you, the customer.

If the store owner recognizes that the bell represents an opportunity to begin building a relationship, he can begin the process of turning a stranger walking through a door into a familiar customer who makes repeat purchases, refers friends, and stays loyal for a long time. If the store owner ignores the bell or fails to make a connection with the person entering the store, the results are likely to be poor. The potential customer is going to remain a stranger who must be convinced again—at great expense—to walk through the same door at a later date.

In email marketing, the bell rings when someone is added to your list. Understanding how to talk to a customer from that point forward using email communications will enable you to tap into the power of relationships and build your business.

Building Customer Relationships with the Constant Contact Cycle

Every once in a while, someone visits your web site or walks through your door and instantly falls in love with your products or services. Unfortunately, a lot of small business owners I talk to are trying to

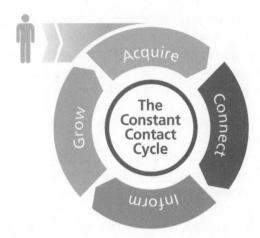

Figure 2.1   The Constant Contact Cycle

survive solely on the small numbers of these "love at first sight" customers. They don't understand how to attract customers from the largest pool of prospective customers—namely the aware but not yet convinced, the skeptics, the comparison shoppers, the indecisive, and the forgetful.

Building a business requires you to convert all kinds of people with all kinds of attitudes into customers and keep them for the long term. That happens when you learn how to build solid customer relationships.

Relationships don't happen overnight; they are built over time. In fact, they typically go through four stages of development. We call these stages the Constant Contact Cycle, shown in Figure 2.1. Maximizing each stage in the cycle is critical to your email marketing.

STAGE ONE—ACQUIRE: THE BEGINNINGS OF A NEW CUSTOMER

Married couples (at least happily married couples) and other people in great relationships like to be asked, "Where did you two meet?" Similarly, you should ask every new prospective customer: "How did you find out about us?"

Before you can start building a high number of lasting relationships, lots of people have to "find out" about you. You have to acquire those relationships in the first place by gaining someone's attention in an initial communication or meeting.

Acquiring new relationships through email is challenging. You can't use email to send your marketing messages to total strangers because people think unfamiliar emails are spam. If your prospects think you're a spammer, that's not going to result in positive or profitable responses to your emails (to read more about spam, flip ahead to Chapter 4). So, you have to acquire new relationships without using email, or by using email to gain referrals at more developed stages of your customer relationships.

Good ways to get people's attention and acquire new relationships include online advertising, search engine marketing, and traditional advertising. After you have earned a potential customer's attention, you can move to stage two of the Constant Contact Cycle and make a connection that's strong enough that they will be willing to give you their contact information.

STEP TWO—CONNECT: FINDING COMMON INTERESTS AND DEMONSTRATING THE VALUE OF YOUR BUSINESS

The second stage in the Constant Contact Cycle is to establish a connection. After you have acquired someone's attention, the connection point happens when you effectively demonstrate the value of your business to your newly acquired prospect. At Constant Contact we call this the "click" point.

What does it mean to click? It means your newly acquired prospect has found something in common with you and is interested in either learning more or continuing to stay in touch after an initial purchase. You'll know when you've "clicked" or "made a connection" when your prospect is willing to share his or her email address by signing up for your email list.

Once you have someone's email address, you can move from higher-cost and less personal "acquisition" advertising and communications to lower-cost and more personal email marketing messages to build customer relationships.

Since demonstrating your value is crucial to making the connections that result in a growing email list, it's important to communicate the value of joining your email list at the first sign of attention. For example, I personally enjoy shopping at small businesses because I like to walk in the door and know that the person I am buying from is truly passionate and knowledgeable about what he is selling. Recently, I walked into a wine store called Vintages in West Concord,

Massachusetts (www.vintagesonline.com). I happened to meet the owner, whose name is Eric, and I told him that I was looking for a special wine for a friend's 50th birthday.

I quickly found out that Eric understands the value of making connections because he jumped up from behind the counter and gave me a quick tour of the wine section of the store. He engaged me in a dialogue to determine my level of interest and knowledge. Then he demonstrated his expertise by discussing the wines that would be worthy of a 50th birthday gift. We settled on a Spanish red and, since I'm an email marketer, I asked Eric if I could sign up for his email list. This took him by surprise, but I suspect he would have asked me if I had not asked first. He told me he would be glad to sign me up and told me that his wife (the co-owner) used Constant Contact to send the emails for the store. He actually had a copy of their most recent email newsletter out on the counter. Now I receive Eric's wine recommendations regularly and I've become a loyal customer.

All this happened because Eric engaged me in a dialogue and listened to my interests before demonstrating his value. I suspect next time I'm in the store looking for a bottle of port, he'll be just as quick to give me a tour of the port section, share his expertise, and start sending me port recommendations.

You don't have to meet people in person to make connections. You can also use your web site, blogs, videos, social media web sites, podcasts, and traditional media to demonstrate your value and ask for email addresses. Just make sure you strive to include as many of the following elements as possible when making connections.

Be Ready to Respond

When your acquisition marketing gets someone's attention, you usually only have one shot to make a connection. For example, your web site needs to be set up to respond to visitors with relevant information and the ability to sign up for more information. At Constant Contact we use different language on our landing pages and our web site depending on what online advertisement our prospects have responded to. That way, we can display more relevant messages to our web site visitors.

If your web site isn't dynamic enough to handle custom messages, you can set up different landing pages for your ads or just give people relevant links so they can quickly find and sign up for the information they are most interested in. To learn more about the tactical ways to obtain email addresses and other information, read Chapter 5.

Engage in a Dialogue

Finding out what your prospects and customers are interested in requires communication both from and to your newly acquired prospects. In the wine store example, this happened in person, but it can also happen online through surveys, trial and error, analytics, and tracking. Be sure to have a couple of standard open-ended questions on hand as conversation starters (e.g., "What type of appliances are you looking for?"). Then once you gain an understanding of the general needs of the customer you can narrow down to their specific needs and interests by asking closed-ended questions (e.g., "Are you interested in gas or electric ranges?").

It's also important to figure out the level of interest and expertise of prospective customers when you engage them in a dialogue. That way, you won't talk over their heads as you demonstrate your knowledge and value.

Demonstrate Your Value in Their Words

The most effective way to demonstrate your value is to acknowledge the specific products or services your prospects and customers find valuable. In the aforementioned wine store example, Eric acknowledged my need for a 50th birthday present, not just a bottle of red wine. This prompted him to share a specific section of his wine store and a specific area of his expertise instead of just showing me the "Expensive Wine" section.

Add Value When Asking to Continue the Dialogue

Asking to continue the dialogue is more than just asking people to join a generic email list. Your email list should be an extension of your business value. In the case of the wine store, I valued Eric's recommendations because I needed a bottle of wine that would be appropriate for an important friend at an important time. If I came into the store looking for a bottle of wine, it might have been more appropriate to ask me to join a "weekly specials" email list.

If you're a medium or large business and your employees are the ones responsible for making connections, it's important to engage your employees and get them thinking about making connections too.

At Constant Contact we put all new employees through "on-boarding training." This training not only provides our employees with an understanding for how our product works but also trains them in how our customers use our products and services to help them succeed in business. By helping our employees understand the many ways our customers use our product, we increase the likelihood that we click with customers on phone calls, through our marketing programs, and through the products that our engineers and product teams create.

A great way to understand how you can start making more connections with your customers is to evaluate the businesses that have made connections with you or your employees. Start by writing down the names of your favorite small businesses or organizations. Then write next to each name what makes the connection special. Is it the way you are treated by their staff, the quality of what they provide, or the contributing role they play in your community? As you look over your list, you will probably notice that there are a lot of different ways that businesses have made a connection with you. You need to be aware of the many potential ways that your customers connect with other businesses so you can identify and encourage any connections you are currently missing.

Another element to think about is how you felt immediately after you made a connection with a business and how long the experience lasted in your memory. Did they follow up on their connection with emails or other communications to extend the experience? Connecting with your customers also includes every positive interaction and exchange that happens after the first interaction. Every future positive connection reaffirms your customer's motivation to continue in the relationship, and every future negative connection reaffirms the possibility that your competition might be a better choice.

When you really connect with a business, the impression lasts. Email marketing, when done right, provides you with the ability to continue the connection. And that brings us to the third stage in the Constant Contact cycle: nurture your connections.

STAGE THREE—NURTURE: CONTINUING THE CONNECTION

The third stage in the Constant Contact Cycle is nurture. Nurturing your relationships keeps your business top-of-mind between purchases and extends the value you create when you acquire new relationships and connect with people. Without nurturing, the value you demonstrated during the process of making a connection will diminish over time, and your prospect or customer will forget all about you or become distracted by your competition's attempts to acquire new relationships through acquisition marketing.

It's commonly known among marketers that it takes six to seven touches to turn a connection into a first-time customer in almost every business. While some people will buy on the very first connection, many with interest will choose to do more research or simply wait a while before making a purchase. Regardless of whether someone purchases from you on the first connection or the tenth, it's important to realize that your stream of ongoing communications must be based on your original connection to effectively nurture your relationships.

In the case of email marketing, it's important to write content that acknowledges your original connection or your emails will become irrelevant and people will unsubscribe from your list before you have a chance to send more than a few messages to them. For example, if you made a connection because someone trusted your expertise, send emails that share more of your expertise versus simply promoting what you offer.

During the 2008 holiday shopping season, many big-box retailers forgot about their customer connections when the economic downturn prompted them to bombard consumers with every email coupon, offer, special, discount, and bundle of value they could think of. At the same time, Constant Contact was advising our customers to continue nurturing their relationships using the same best-practices that worked before the economic downturn. The results were made obvious in a joint report by eMarketer and ReturnPath that showed 98.6 percent of consumers felt they received too many emails over the holidays. More than 30 percent of respondents said the emails were junk and 60 percent said they just deleted unfamiliar and unwanted emails. What's more, just over 33 percent of respondents said the emails had no impact on their holiday spending.

Kitchen Outfitters (www.kitchen-outfitters.com; see Figure 2.2) rallied all of the other store owners in its strip mall through a customer appreciation event on a Sunday afternoon leading

Figure 2.2   Kitchen Outfitters rallies local stores to drive holiday sales.

up to the holidays. By banding together neighboring stores along with expert musicians from a local music school, Kitchen Outfitters was able to attract a large audience, engage their local community, drive significant foot traffic, and generate business—defying the odds at a time when every sale mattered.

Knowing what I know about email marketing, I guarantee these emails not only failed to nurture the connections the retailers made into more purchases during the holidays, they also made it more difficult—if not impossible—for these retailers to nurture their connections into a relationship of trust, which is the fourth and most valuable stage of the Constant Contact Cycle.

STAGE FOUR—TRUST: THE END AND THE BEGINNING

Acquiring, connecting, and nurturing correctly will result in many valuable business relationships, but the most valuable business relationships have the added element of trust. The reason trust is so valuable is because trusting customers begin to value their relationship with your business as much as you value your relationship with them and their patronage.

The first act of trust actually happens during the connection stage of the Constant Contact Cycle, because someone has to trust you enough to share his or her email address with you. The kind of trust that is present in the fourth stage of the Constant Contact Cycle is much deeper, however.

It develops over the course of many email communications, personal interactions, and time. The number of emails is less important than the types of emails you send. The more targeted, relevant, and valuable the information you are sending, the more trust will develop in your relationships. Also, the more time your customers spend on your email list receiving your emails without unsubscribing, the more trust will develop in your relationships.

Trust is extremely valuable to your business. Customers who trust you are more willing to respond to your email promotions. That means you'll motivate more purchases per email in a trusting audience than in an audience of new connections. It's possible for a business to survive solely on repeat business from a trusting customer base because of the higher response rates, but the business has to build up enough trusting customers to generate a sustainable amount of purchases per email. More purchases per email also translates into less time, money, energy, and effort spent creating acquisition marketing to attract new customers into the cycle. If you can sustain and grow your business on trust, you'll also acquire new relationships through referrals.

This brings me to the second result of trust: Trusting customers are more willing to refer your business to their friends and colleagues. People who refer your business to others are putting their reputation on the line for your business. The more trust you develop in your relationships, the more referrals you're going to get. When trusting customers refer you to others, they are starting the Constant Contact Cycle for you all over again by helping you acquire a new relationship at nearly zero cost to you.

One of the most powerful things about email marketing is that it's easy to forward an email message on to others. In fact, the Forward Button in your email program is a constant reminder to your customers that they can share your message with others.

Trust Pays Dividends

I took several of our customers out to dinner in Los Gatos, California, a number of years ago to get a better understanding for how email marketing had impacted their businesses. One of the participants told the group about his first encounter with Constant Contact. He ran a business that helped companies that were relocating with furniture and fixtures and he had a list of roughly 1,400 trusting customers. When he sent his first email, it resulted in a six-figure sale. That would have been a great story all by itself, but the story was even more compelling when he stated that the sale was not made to anyone on the email list but rather to someone who received the email as a forward from someone on the list. Now that's trust really paying dividends!

Four Examples and Rewards of Running a Relationship Business

Great customer relationships that develop into trust define the health and growth potential of your business. Trust results in repeat business and referrals, and there are also many other rewards associated with strong relationships.

The following sections provide four windows into the kinds of benefits you can expect in return when you focus your email marketing on building toward trust instead of just promoting transactions. Each section includes a benefit and a real-life example of a business that has derived the benefit using email marketing to develop trust.

These are the same benefits we strive for at Constant Contact, and they have made us very successful. Use our experience, and the following examples, as a guide so you can start recognizing and building valuable relationships of your own through your email marketing.

YOU'RE FIRST

When you invest in building relationships with your customers, they return the favor by thinking of you first when the time comes for making a purchase. Customers who have a relationship with you will also go out of their way and ignore the competition.

I lived in New York City in the late 1980s, and at that time I began shopping for clothing at a men's clothing store called Rothman's. The store offers high-quality clothing at reasonable prices with the added benefit of store employees who really go out of their way to provide their customers with a great shopping experience (see Figure 2.3). Over time, the store owner, Ken Giddon, and I became good friends because he made every shopping experience special and nurtured our relationship with ongoing relevant and valuable communications. To this day, when it comes to shopping for clothing, I put most purchases on hold until travel takes me from Acton, Massachusetts, to New York where I do all my shopping at Rothmans.

Email marketing is not only about trying to sell more product, it's also about extending the shopping experience and building trust. Rothmans' email marketing campaigns continue the Rothmans experience by sharing tips on men's fashion, advice on how to select a well-made suit, or ways to spruce up an old suit with a new shirt and tie. The emails not only build trust, they make their customers think of them first and foremost.

PRICE IS PETTY

Customers who value your relationship are less price-sensitive than customers who only value the transaction. That doesn't mean you can charge anything you want for your products or services, and it certainly doesn't mean you should reward loyal customers with higher prices. What it does mean is you won't have to spend too much of your valuable time bargaining with customers or worrying too much about how your competition is pricing their products and services.

I have one of those major home supply stores right by my office, but I prefer to go to the local Acton ACE hardware store for most of my hardware needs. The primary reason is the connection I have with the people who work there. I realize that I am probably paying a little more for a certain piece of hardware; however, they take the time to find me when I walk in the door and ask me what I am looking for, versus the major home supply store where I spend half my time in the store trying to find someone who knows where the stuff is that I need. Time is money, and it's more important for me to quickly find what I am looking for than for me to save 20 percent on a box of nails, and in addition it feels great to be able to support our local business community.

Figure 2.3   Rothman's extends the shopping experience.

CUSTOMERS RETURN MORE OFTEN

The stronger your relationships, the easier it will become to draw your customers back to your business. Repeat business usually starts out of familiarity or convenience, and then grows as trust develops. When you develop trust, your repeat business starts to come from a sense of obligation or even emotional attachment. Those feelings are valuable to your business because they generate very loyal customers. They are also very fragile, however. When you have relationships of trust in your business, be extra careful not to take advantage of those relationships and make sure you are thanking your loyal customers often.

Il Forno is my family's favorite local go-to restaurant. Whenever we talk about going out for dinner, it is the first restaurant that comes to mind. It's our first pick because the food is great, and more importantly, the wait staff recognize us when we walk in the door. In fact, it was actually the actions of one employee, Jenn, that won us over on our first visit. She learned the names of our children, asked us what we wanted for dinner, and had the kitchen create her favorite salad, which was not on the menu. She also made sure to welcome us back each time we returned to the restaurant. When you have this type of relationship, email marketing is all about making your audience feel like part of your family.

CUSTOMERS SPREAD THE WORD

When you develop trust in your relationships, you're going to get more direct referrals, and your customers are going to spread the word about your business without giving you a direct referral.

Here's how it works: It comes down to basic human nature. When your customers trust you and frequent your business, they will share stories about their interactions with you through the course of normal human interaction. It's human nature to want to be perceived as being smart, connected, and knowledgeable. People will talk about your business with friends, colleagues, and co-workers because they like to share knowledge that adds value to conversations. Your job as an email marketer is to make sure your customers have knowledge that is worth sharing with others. At Constant Contact we have learned that leads that come from our existing customers convert at the highest rates of any of our new customer sources. There is nothing like

Figure 2.4   Flyte shares knowledge with its audience.

one business owner saying to another, "You should be using Constant Contact."

Flyte news media's (www.flyte.biz) "flyte log" newsletter contains a wealth of information on how to succeed online (see Figure 2.4). In this edition, the company president and author, Rich Brooks, dedicates the entire body of the communication to helping his readers learn how to leverage online video for fun and profit. In sharing his knowledge with his readers, Rich is not only reinforcing his reputation as an expert in the space, he's also greatly increasing the likelihood that his readers will share their newfound source of great knowledge with others.

When I ask business owners where the majority of their business is going to come from in the next month or quarter, the reply I typically receive is "from my existing customers." At this point I usually borrow a quote from Warren Buffett, who said "In the business world the rear view mirror is always clearer than the windshield." While I am not sure of the context of Mr. Buffett's statement, the point is that by focusing your attention on the satisfied customer walking out the door you will find a clearer path to success. Harnessing the power of relationships is all about tapping into the rear view mirror through ongoing communications with people that already know who you are. In the next chapter we will explore why email marketing is the most cost-effective way to continue an ongoing conversation with your customers.

3

Making Money: The Economics of Email

I live close to a golf course, so my garage is always full of golf balls collected by my children. We literally have big plastic containers filled with golf balls sorted by type and condition. While I like to keep a container with the best of them in my trunk to meet my endless need, my children have other ideas.

Mitchell and Madeline, who seem to have the same entrepreneurial spirit I have, would rather sell these balls back to the golfers as they drive by our house on their way home.

The reality is, turning a profit on free golf balls might prove less profitable than they hope. After all, attracting people to a curbside store will require a communication strategy. They'll need to buy a sign to put in the yard, and since not everyone lives on our street, they may have to place an ad in the country club newsletter to let people know when they'll be in the yard, get the other neighbors to drive by our house, and explain why it's worth driving out of their way for some used golf balls.

If they aren't careful, they might end up spending more money to advertise the golf balls than the value of their time spent acquiring them in the first place. A lot of small business owners make the same mistake. In order to be profitable, marketing communications have to result in more money taken in than they cost.

This chapter explains how to efficiently use email marketing to make sure the money you spend on all your marketing efforts generates enough money for your business.

How to Maximize the Return on Your Email Marketing Dollars

Depending on which study you read, it can take six to seven interactions to turn a prospective customer into a first-time customer. Many of the business owners who come to Constant Contact seeking higher returns on their marketing dollars quickly realize that higher returns happen when they stop focusing so heavily on acquiring new customers and spend more time communicating effectively after the initial touch.

IDENTIFYING YOUR CUSTOMER TOUCH POINTS

Figuring out where your customers come from helps you determine where to invest your money and where to cut unprofitable spending. In case you think you know exactly where your customers come from, consider the following example:

Sally, a small business owner with a brick-and-mortar jewelry store, is contemplating stopping sending emails because most of her new customers were coming from the online ads she places on Google when people search for "jewelry store in Omaha, NE."

When Sally asks her new customers how they found out about her, they say they searched online and found her web site. However, if she had conducted further investigation, she would have found that her new customers actually come from her emails and several other touch points.

For example, she asks people to join her email list at the networking events she attends each week. These prospective customers are receiving her emails, but they aren't always ready to buy jewelry immediately when the emails go out.

When Sally's customers are ready to buy, they remember the networking event, the emails, and the town her store is in, but they don't remember the name of her store or exactly where it's located. So, they search for "jewelry store in Omaha, NE" to find out where the store is and when she is open.

Then they drive to Sally's store, which happens to be across the street from another jewelry store. Since the sign over her store looks the same as the logo on her web site, Sally's customers are able to track her down easily. However, if Sally were to ask customers how they found her, she would be just as likely to hear from a web search, yellow pages, or the sign on the door as she would be to hear the real source—her networking efforts. This simple example highlights the challenges of figuring out which of your marketing efforts drives the greatest return for your business. That said, the more you know about your sources, the more effective you can be in maximizing your spend.

The combination of your marketing media is known as the *marketing mix,* and it's important to understand the role each touch point plays in driving business your way.

When I work with business owners on maximizing their email marketing spend, I often start by assessing their overall marketing strategy. I start here because email marketing is a critical component of a comprehensive marketing strategy and it needs to be interwoven with every other marketing program being deployed. I typically start the marketing strategy discussion with a conversation on the market opportunity, during which I ask three questions:

1. Define your target market. What are the characteristics of your most likely customers (age, gender, location, interests, business types, etc.)?

2. How do they congregate (where, with whom, when, etc.)?

3. How do you plan to reach them (directly, indirectly, word of mouth, etc.)?

This is followed by a discussion of where the business owners believe their revenue will come from over the next 24 months. I ask them to answer this question by allocating a percentage of the total future revenue into one of three buckets:

1. **The Unaware.** people or businesses that have no idea who you are today

2. **The Aware.** people or businesses that know of you today but are not a customer

3. **The Active.** people or businesses that have already purchased from you

Simply put, the ultimate goal of your marketing strategy is to make the unaware aware, drive the aware to become active, and get the active to return on a regular basis. To maximize your marketing mix,

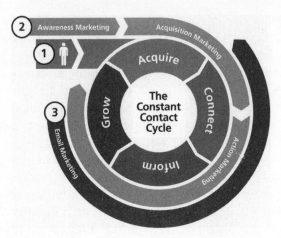

Figure 3.1   Constant Contact Cycle with Marketing Mix

you simply need to determine the most cost-effective way to move people from one stage to the next and then determine how much of your budgeted time and dollars you want to allocate to each step.

I often use Figure 3.1 to demonstrate the correlation between the Constant Contact Cycle and the components of a well defined marketing strategy, and the role email marketing plays to point out how they are interdependent and aligned.

The inner ring (1) of the diagram is the process through which relationships are formed, starting with acquisition and leading ultimately to trust. At each stage of the cycle it is important to understand that different marketing strategies are needed in order to move a customer from one stage to the next. The second ring (2) highlights these strategies and they are more fully defined below. The final ring (3) represents the role of email marketing and the typical path that it takes as it is integrated into the overall marketing mix. You will note that it starts at point 3 (Grow Stage), with email being sent to engage existing customers, and then migrates back towards acquire as it is deployed to help in converting prospects to customers and ultimately into an acquisition vehicle as recipients forward your communications on to others.

A well designed email marketing strategy acts as grease that speeds up the customer relationship cycle (Ring 1). In looking at the chart above, it's interesting to note that businesses typically think marketing focuses solely on moving the aware to action (Acquisition Marketing). As we will explore in subsequent chapters, a well structured email marketing strategy typically starts with getting repeat business from those who have already purchased from you (Action Marketing), but then naturally migrates back around to enhance Acquisition Marketing efforts and ultimately drive awareness.

Before you dive into the process of determining your marketing allocation, it's worthwhile to evaluate the characteristics of the marketing mix available to you at each stage in the process. This will help you balance your investments and maximize the velocity at which the cycle spins.

Stage One: Awareness Marketing: *The Process of Making People Aware that You Exist*

The key to Awareness Marketing success is understanding your target market. The narrower you can define your market, the easier it will be to determine the most suitable marketing medium to use. For example, for a plumber this might be the yellow pages, for a coffee shop it might be as simple as having a great looking sign and being in the right location, for a non-profit it might be getting coverage by the local press. Awareness Marketing programs tend to be the most expensive type of marketing you will do for your business. This is due, in part, to the fact that it is often difficult to track the return on your marketing investment. At Constant Contact, we consider our national radio campaign to be an Awareness Marketing campaign. Email marketing is not a marketing medium that is typically thought about as something used to create awareness. However, if you do email marketing well, awareness can be generated through word-of-mouth referrals.

Stage Two: Acquisition Marketing: *The Process of Driving the Aware to Take Action*

This form of marketing is typically easier to track than awareness marketing. At Constant Contact, we consider the marketing efforts that drive traffic to our web site to be Acquisition Marketing and we track each source based on volume, quality, and longevity. This enables us to determine the best places for us to invest to drive new business.

The key element associated with this type of marketing is that there is a clear direction you want the prospective customer to take. Whether it is to your web site, storefront, or an event, the path is clear and traceable. Email marketing plays an integral role in acquisition marketing because once you've established a connection, it is the most cost effective way for you to communicate and nurture the connection into a first time customer.

Stage Three: Action Marketing: *The Process of Getting the Active to Return on a Regular Basis*

Once you have invested in acquiring a customer, you have done all the heavy lifting from an investment standpoint. Now it's up to you to continue to remind your customers of the value you provide so they continue to return to you when they need what you provide. This is truly the sweet spot of email marketing. By regularly delivering professional communications that contain information the recipient finds valuable, you will maximize the revenue potential of your customers, maximize the return on investment of all your other marketing investments, and likely reap the added benefit of word-of-mouth marketing as your customers forward your message on to their friends and family.

Now it's time to take out a piece of paper and write down your marketing strategy. Be sure to list every place you interact with your customers and prospective customers. This is something you will want to update regularly. It will give you a great starting point for determining how to incorporate email marketing into your overall mix.

FIGURING OUT HOW MUCH TO INVEST

Spending money on marketing is going to feel a lot more like an expense than an investment if you rely too heavily on using paid mass messages to turn total strangers into customers. In fact, the economics of a successful marketing mix are derived from your ability to invest in the most effective messaging *after* one of your first touch points grabs the attention of a total stranger. Compare the following two scenarios with the same starting economics, as shown in Table 3.1.

Let's say you decide to spend $500 on a paid mass advertisement that results in ten people walking into your store. Out of ten people:

♦ Two have an immediate need for what you sell and will make a $100 purchase

♦ Six are potential future buyers

♦ Two aren't interested in your business at all.

Table 3.1 Two Marketing Scenarios

Scenario	Spend ($)	Prospects	Sales ($)	Interest	No Interest	Contact Info	Added Sales ($)
1	500	10	200	6	2	0	0
2	500	10	200	6	2	6	400

Scenario 1: You sell your product to the two with an immediate need and make $200. Since you spent $500 on the ad, the net cost to you was $300 to generate those sales. If you want to get more customers in the store, you could run another $500 ad and lose another $300, or you can do what I recommend by following Scenario 2.

Scenario 2: You sell your product to the two with an immediate need and you make $200. You also make a good enough impression on four of the other six that they are willing to share their email addresses. If you also get contact information from the two customers, you now have contact information for six new prospects.

At this point, you have experienced the same economics as Scenario 1, but you no longer have to spend $500 to get more customers in the store because you can send your email newsletter and email promotions as a follow up to the people who shared their email addresses. Of course, this will cost you much less. (As an example, Constant Contact allows you to send as many emails as you want, up to 500 people, for $15.00 per month.)

If your follow-up emails result in one of the two customers coming back to make a purchase and three of the six interested prospects coming back to make a purchase, the four new purchases will result in $400 in added sales, and you will now have a profit of $100 instead of a $300 loss, minus the low costs of your email program.

Having a communications strategy can not only help you generate additional revenue from your marketing efforts, it can actually change the economics so that investments that make no sense alone can actually become profitable when looked at collectively.

Figuring out how much to invest isn't about assigning a percentage of your budget to advertising, it's about making investments in messages that work together to live beyond the first touch. In the next section I'll explain where to invest.

CUTTING THE FAT AND MAXIMIZING YOUR INVESTMENTS

Now it's time for a little math. You need to find out the cost of acquisition (COA) for each customer source so you can determine whether you need to cut a cost, apply a lower cost messaging strategy to an upfront cost, or invest more in the same cost.

The cost of acquisition is a fancy way of asking, "How much do I have to invest in a given source for it to generate a new customer?" Here is the formula:

$$COA = \frac{\text{Amount spent}}{\text{The number of customers generated}}$$

Example using Direct Mail:

$$\frac{\$10,000 \, \text{Amount spent on } 10,000 \, \text{pieces (annually)}}{100 \, \text{Number of customers generated (annually)}} = \$100 \, COA$$

Take out a piece of paper and calculate the COA for each of your customer touch points. For now, leave out email marketing. Once you have a COA for each source, list them on a piece of paper from highest to lowest. Table 3.2 shows an example.

This summary highlights the magnitude and productivity of each of your marketing investments. Whether you have additional money to spend on marketing your business or are looking to re-balance your current spending to maximize your return, this approach provides you with the information you need to make the right decisions.

However, before you start slashing costs or investing more, it is equally important to do some re-weighting of your results based on the quality and quantity of the leads generated from each source.

Table 3.2 Example COA Without Email Marketing

Type of Ad	Cost ($)	Customers	COA ($)
Newspaper Ads:	15,000	75	200
Direct Mail:	10,000	100	100
Directory Listing:	5,000	50	100
Improved Web Site:	5,000	50	100
Search Advertising:	5,000	100	50
Word-of-Mouth Referrals:	0	25	0
Totals:	40,000	400	100 (avg)

Table 3.3 Example COA with Email Marketing Lead Nurture

Type of Ad	Cost ($)	Customers	COA ($)	Leads
Newspaper Ads:	15,000	75	200	500
Direct Mail:	10,000	100	100	250
Directory Listing:	5,000	50	100	500
Improved Web Site:	5,000	50	100	500
Search Advertising:	5,000	100	50	750
Word-of-Mouth Referrals:	0	25	0	250
Email Marketing*:	500	275*	1.80	0
Totals:	40,500	675	60	2,750*

* assumes that email marketing can convert 10 percent of your leads into future customers. Though I can't share our conversion rate at Constant Contact, I can assure you that our rate is much higher than that.

In the example above, it would be easy to make the case to eliminate the newspaper ad since it is clearly the most expensive source of customers. However, if your newspaper ad runs in a highly targeted publication and you receive 500 quality leads from that ad per year, you might be able to justify the expense if you find a way to convert those leads at a lower cost using email marketing. An example of this is shown in Table 3.3.

Note that acquiring 275 additional customers for only $1.80 each brings the total cost of acquisition down by 40 percent from $100 each to $60 each. In this case, it might make more sense to cut your direct mail and invest that money in more newspaper or search ads.

The quality of your leads and the contact information you receive has a direct impact on your ability to convert those customers. Poor quality leads could increase your costs or eliminate your ability to convert anyone to a customer.

For example, if you have a shoe store and the search engine ad in the table above reflects visitors who searched for "hiking boots," you shouldn't count those visitors as quality leads unless you are sure they were potential customers trying to buy hiking boots instead of high school students writing reports on camping gear.

Usually you need to collect some identifying information to count someone as a lead, and the quality of that information impacts your ability to follow up in a meaningful way.

How do you attract new customers?

Type of promotion	Amount spent per year	÷	New customers per year	=	Cost per customer
Yellow Pages Ads	_____		_____		_____
Radio	_____		_____		_____
Print (Newspaper)	_____		_____		_____
Online Marketing	_____		_____		_____
Direct Mail	_____		_____		_____
Leads Groups	_____		_____		_____
Organizations	_____		_____		_____
Other	_____		_____		_____
Total cost per customer	_____		_____		_____
	(A)	÷	(B)	=	(C)

How much profit do you generate from a typical sale?

_____ (P)

Calculate how many purchases it will take for you to "break even" on a new customer.

For example: If your total cost per new customer is $100 and your profit per typical sale is $20, it will take you five sales until you break even (100 ÷ 20 = 5).

Total cost per customer:	Profit from a typical sale:	Number of purchases to break-even:
(C) _____	÷ (P) _____	= _____

Figure 3.2   COA and Break-Even Analysis

All these examples point to one thing: If you can follow up multiple times at a low cost, you'll gain more customers and spend less money in the long run. Figure 3.2 shows a form that you can use to figure out your own Cost of Acquisition and the number of purchases needed to break even on a new customer. If you would like to download this table along with the rest of Constant Contact's Email Marketing Workbook visit www.constantcontact.com/workbook.

Once you've identified places to cut or invest, spend some time thinking about non-monetary ways you can impact the number of leads you generate from each source. For example, you can stimulate word-of-mouth and referrals by asking for them instead of waiting for them.

From my experience at Constant Contact, I can say that trying to stimulate word-of-mouth is difficult to accomplish by investing money in gifts and expensive programs. Customers who refer you to others are putting their reputation on the line for your business, and that is something, for most people, that cannot be bought. However, it can be *encouraged* by simply telling people at the bottom of your email that you appreciate it when people refer your business to others and inviting them to forward your email to one or two other people who might find the content interesting.

It's also a good idea to use some of the money you cut from your marketing budget to invest in experimentation. Once you know what you are currently paying to attract new customers, you are well positioned to not only optimize the return you generate from these sources, but to negotiate with new sources.

At Constant Contact our marketing mantra is "test, then invest." We are open to trying any marketing program that reliably reaches our customer demographic and is something that we can measure. However, we first test it on a small scale in order to determine that it generates new customers within our cost tolerances. If it performs, then we scale it accordingly.

In all cases, make sure your communications provide all interested prospective customers with a way to continue the dialogue in a way that provides you with a low-cost connection.

Reaping the Soft Benefits of Email Marketing

In addition to the direct financial benefits of email marketing, there are a number of other financial benefits that are difficult to track. For example, if your logo appears in an email, you might not see sales from people who drove right over to your store to make a purchase, but it might make your web site seem more familiar to a visitor who has seen the email, and that might make her more comfortable making a purchase at a later date.

These kinds of benefits are known as *soft benefits*. I can tell you firsthand that soft benefits translate into financial impact, and I can also tell you that you shouldn't spend any time or money trying to emulate the big money branding strategies you see from large companies in hopes of receiving soft benefits in return.

The right approach to soft benefits is to pay attention to them and let them happen while you're pursuing measurable direct-response communications. The next sections explain many of the soft benefits you can derive at a low cost while you're gaining from the more direct benefits of your email marketing strategy.

TOP-OF-MIND AWARENESS

Have you ever spent a lot of time with potential customers teaching them about your products or services, only to find out that they made a purchase from someone else? When you hang up the phone or the customer walks out the door of your office or leaves your web site, the opportunity to stay "top-of-mind" with your customer starts to diminish. The more time that elapses, the greater the likelihood that the customer will forget all about the services or products you offer.

It happens to everyone at one time or another because even people with the best intentions make purchase decisions based on being in close proximity to an offer at the precise time when they are ready to make a purchase. When you send professional-looking email communications, you remind your audience that you exist and you're ready to serve them when they need you.

Top-of-mind awareness also helps you gain referrals. When one of your customers gives a referral, he or she is likely to share the first few businesses that come to mind. If you're in front of your customers with regular email communications, you're more likely to be at the top of the list.

Competition among hotels on Cape Cod is high due to the tourist-based, seasonal nature of the region. As the proprietor of the Crowne Pointe Historic Inn and Spa, David Sanford wanted customers to think of his hotel as a signature Provincetown destination twelve months a year (see Figure 3.3). David abandoned his traditional marketing approach in favor of email marketing, which enabled him to regularly reach out to customers in a timely, inexpensive way that captured Crowne Pointe's elegant brand. He sends monthly updates about hotel, spa, and restaurant promotions to his list. As a result of his efforts, he has been able to greatly improve year-round attendance at special and promotional events.

There are two ways you can improve your ability to bring your customers back: customer loyalty (developed over time through a buildup of trust) and contact information (which provides you with the ability to maintain regular contact).

In the case of new customers or prospective customers, you have not yet had a chance to build up trust, so the ability to maintain contact

Figure 3.3   Crowne Pointe Inn stays top-of-mind with professional-looking campaigns.

is even more important. When it comes to customers with whom you have a lot of existing loyalty, email marketing works to "tap them on the shoulder" and say, "Do you need my services this month?" and "Do you have any friends who might?"

HEIGHTENED BRAND IDENTITY

Your customers need to be able to distinguish you from the competition and feel confident in your ability to provide what they need. The more times someone sees your logo, business name, colors, and other identifying features of your business, the more confident they will feel that your business is legitimate.

If you're a small business, you don't need everyone to be able to draw your logo from memory, but you do need to make your business familiar to your audience. The best way to do that is by repeating the same brand elements in a consistent way.

Building an identity also increases the response rates from your other marketing efforts when you use consistent branding (see Figure 3.4).

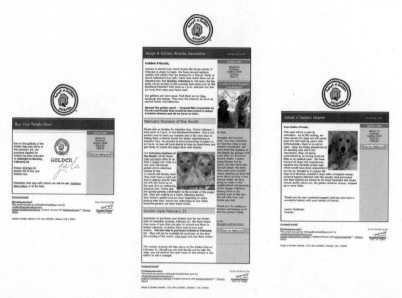

Figure 3.4   Building an identity with email involves consistent branding across all communications.

INCREASED CUSTOMER LOYALTY

Loyal customers will bypass the competition on the way to your store, office, or web site, because they trust you more than they trust the competition. Customer loyalty can be built through your email communications when you communicate your desire to continue the relationship with your customers after making a purchase.

For example, compare a used car dealer who sells you a faulty car and disappears with a used car dealer who sells the same faulty car but sends a follow up email asking for your feedback and is willing to correct the problem when your response points to a disrepair.

Loyalty results in more frequent purchases, higher purchases per transaction, and other benefits that aren't necessarily tied to the number or cost of communications you send.

There are three major takeaway points when it comes to understanding the economics of email marketing. First, email marketing is not a standalone marketing strategy. It works in concert with all your other marketing efforts. Second, when done right, email marketing will make all your other marketing investments more effective. Finally, email marketing is most effective in helping you stay relevant and connected with the people that already know what you have to offer.

4

The Benefits of Permission-Based Email Marketing

Email marketing is a very inexpensive way to communicate. Not surprisingly, some misguided people think that the low cost of sending a message gives them the right to blast their message out to everyone with an email address.

If I had to choose one thing that was the key to Constant Contact's success in the early days, I would probably say that we were the first email marketing company to take the issue of permission-based marketing very seriously. Constant Contact was an advocate for permission marketing in 1998, one year before Seth Godin's famed book on the subject. Obviously, we weren't the only ones who knew the power of permission.

In 2001, we tested offering a list rental service through one of the most reputable list rental companies in the business. We quickly shut down this test when our customers gave us feedback that the results they were experiencing were horrible. I can honestly say that we would be doing our customers a tremendous disservice today if we allowed them to buy or rent email lists.

This chapter explains how and why your reputation is on the line with every email that you send, and helps you to make sure every impression you make is a positive one.

Is Your Email Glamorous or Spam-orous?

Sending an email to someone who doesn't know you is like putting up a sign in a storefront window that says: "Don't Do Business with Me!" Whether your email is glamorous, because it is loved by your recipients, or "spam-orous" because it is perceived as spam by your recipients, is a legal, professional, and personal matter.

It's a legal matter because laws protect consumers from unsolicited email. It's a professional matter because the Internet and email industries expect businesses to adhere to best practices. It's a personal matter because ultimately your customers are the ones who determine what is spam and what is not. Quite simply, if they think your email is spam, then it's spam.

The following sections explain the personal issues related to spam. I cover the legal and professional issues a little later on.

WHY CONSUMERS—NOT SENDERS—GET TO DECIDE WHAT SPAM IS

Your definition of spam doesn't matter, and neither does mine, unless we define it in exactly the same way as our recipients define it. The ultimate judge and jury when it comes to spam is the recipient of the message, not the sender.

Consumers think spam is anything they don't want or can't verify. If they don't want it, they think it's spam. If they don't know who it's from, they think it's spam.

As a sender, you need to recognize that your recipient's inbox is his or her property. The average consumer considers spam an invasion of privacy—trespassing, if you will. Put yourself in your recipient's inbox. How do you react when you receive email from someone you don't know and don't trust? Immediate delete. Why? Because that person is wasting your time and violating your privacy.

When you ask for someone's email address and permission, you are asking to take some of his time and attention. When someone provides her email address, she is telling you that she respects you enough to give you something of value to her—her time and attention.

THE DANGERS OF TOO MANY SPAM COMPLAINTS

Sending email to total strangers will result in spam complaints. You should be very concerned with how many spam complaints you receive, because they have the ability to ruin your email marketing strategy. There are four reasons why you should do everything possible to avoid spam complaints.

1. Your Reputation Is Tarnished.

When people think your email is spam and your logo and business's name appears in the email, they associate your business with those nasty spammers. If you were to send a bunch of postcards through the mail and nobody wanted them, people would just throw them away. But, if you were to send a bunch of emails through an Email Service Provider and nobody wanted them, people would hoot, holler, complain, and get enraged. Consumers really dislike spam.

2. Your Emails Get Blocked or Filtered.

Internet Service Providers (ISPs) like Yahoo!, AOL, and MSN are in business to deliver the emails their customers want, while keeping the emails they don't want from getting to their inboxes. So they spend millions of dollars and countless resources trying to deliver good email while filtering and blocking the bad email.

ISPs keep track of senders who get too many spam complaints by registering the domain name and IP address of the senders who receive the complaints. Don't let it bother you—that is, unless you receive more than one spam complaint in every 1,000 emails. After that, you'll start to see those complaints negatively impact your reputation with ISPs and ESPs. Once your reputation is tarnished, your email is more likely to be filtered or blocked by the ISPs.

3. You Get Tossed from Email Service Providers.

ESPs like Constant Contact send their customers' emails from email servers owned by the ESP. In order to keep a good reputation with ISPs, ESPs need to help their customers keep their spam complaints low. Spam complaints directed at ESP customers are logged against the ESP, not the ESP's customer.

ESP customers who receive too many complaints and are unwilling to take measures to reduce the complaints are shut down to protect the rest of the ESP's customers and their ability to deliver email to ISPs at the highest possible rate.

4. Your Customers Won't Come Back

When someone complains that your email is spam, you're probably going to lose a customer for one of two reasons. First, your email probably isn't going to get delivered to that customer's inbox again, so your customer won't receive the newsletters, promotions, or event invitations you work so hard to create. Second, your customer isn't likely to be impressed with your business. If you're perceived as a spammer, you're like an annoying menace instead of a trusted friend.

AVOIDING SPAM COMPLAINTS ENTIRELY ISN'T POSSIBLE, BUT MINIMIZING THEM IS

Reporting email as spam can be as easy as clicking the "This is Spam" button in your email client (as shown in Figure 4.1), or as involved as finding the source of the email in the message headers and reporting that email as spam to the listed owner of the IP address. The public can also report unsolicited email to third-party reporting services, such as SpamCop and SpamHaus.

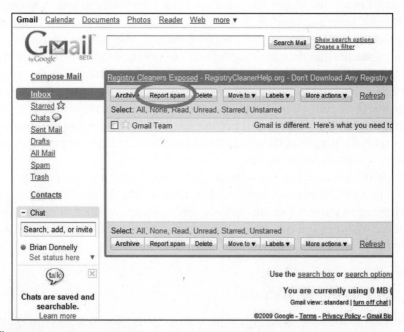

Figure 4.1 The spam button allows consumers to easily report spam emails.

Since spam complaints are often a matter of opinion, they are some-times triggered by factors that are out of your control. Even if you're a permission-based email marketer, if you wait long enough, you'll get a few spam complaints. Sometimes you'll even get them—albeit inadvertently—from your friends, relatives, and life-long customers.

Within Constant Contact we provide our customers with feedback in the event that one of their recipients reports an email as spam. Receiving a spam complaint from someone who is supposed to know you and your business might feel like you're being betrayed by a friend, especially when you've worked so hard to build a permission-based list. You are following the rules, so why the spam complaint?

It may be that certain characteristics of your email look like spam to your subscribers or they aren't satisfied with what they are getting from you. But take heart: There are ways to help more of your recipients respond with approval instead of with the spam button.

HOW TO LOOK PROFESSIONAL IN A HOSTILE INBOX ENVIRONMENT

The best way to look professional to your audience is to become an email critic and study what comes into your own inbox. I suggest creating several email folders, one for email that stands out from all others and positively impacts your opinion of the sender, and another for messages that make you never want to do business with a company.

Over time, you may find reasons to create sub-folders for great subject lines, beautiful templates, and great calls to action. However, for starters, two should suffice. Leverage the best of the best as you create your campaigns, and before you schedule the campaign to be sent, check it against the characteristics of the bad campaigns to make sure you stand out from the crowd.

Still, there are some common elements that can cause consumers to pull the spam-complaint trigger that might go unnoticed when you're reviewing the emails in your inbox. Here are the five most com-mon consumer spam-complaint triggers and how you can avoid pulling them.

1. Questionable Identity

Clearly communicating your identity is the number one way to avoid spam complaints. According to a survey by the Email Sender and Provider Coalition, 79 percent of consumers clicked the spam button when they didn't know who the sender was. Here are the two simplest ways to make your identity apparent.

- **Use a familiar name in your "From" line.** Use the same words your audience uses to identify you or your business. For example, if you're an online business and your customers refer to you by your domain name instead of your formal business name, put your domain name in your From line. If you are your brand, and everyone on your list knows who you are, use your name. An example of a well formatted From line would be rothmans@rothmansny.com, while one at the other end of the spectrum might look like this: info1435349@gmail.com.

- **Include your brand.** Insert your logo into the upper left or center of every email and include image descriptions (alt. text) for readers who have images disabled. Choose colors that identify your business when designing your email templates and use the same colors in every template you use. Don't just use the stock template colors.

2. Irrelevant Content

Consumers expect their email subscriptions to deliver value. According to eMarketer, 46 percent of Internet users say the commercial emails they receive are not targeted to their needs. Since your email list is likely to include people with a variety of interests, take these interests into account before you send.

- **Offer choices on your sign-up form.** Some consumers want to receive promotions, while others only want informative newsletters. Offering options helps you make your emails relevant.

- **Use click-through data to target future messages.** When people click on your links, they tell you what they are interested in. Use this data to create different email lists.

- **Send surveys and polls to learn about preferences.** Instead of making assumptions about what to send, ask. You can conduct a formal survey before starting a major email campaign or use ongoing polls to get small bits of information over time and adjust your strategy as you go.

Figure 4.2   Welcome emails help you to reinforce and match the interests of new subscribers.

3. Broken Promises

Sending emails that your subscribers didn't ask for (i.e., promotions when they signed up for an email newsletter) can be perceived by your audience as a broken promise. Give your subscribers clear expectations before they share their email addresses, then keep your promises.

◆ **Tell your new subscribers what you're going to send.** Clearly describe each type of email communication you offer (e.g., promotions, newsletters, event announcements) and ask new subscribers which they would like to receive.

Send a welcome email after new subscribers join. Whether they join through your web site or you add them to your list after they subscribe offline, send a welcome email that clearly describes the email content you plan to send. You can also send welcome emails after your audience has received a few of your emails to make sure they are happy and receiving the right information (see Figure 4.2).

4. Excessive Promotion

Selling your products or services is an important part of your email marketing, but, according to a Jupiter Research survey, 40 percent of consumers said they stopped subscribing to opt-in emails because they were getting too many offers. Sending promotions too frequently might lead to spam complaints.

♦ **Keep your promotional frequency in line with your business model.** If you sell items that are consumed quickly, your audience probably expects more frequent promotions than if you sell items that are normally purchased every few months, years, or once in a lifetime.

♦ **Place promotions on your web site and use informative email content to drive clicks.** Instead of putting an entire article and a promotion in your email newsletter, use only the first two or three sentences in your email and post the rest of the article, and a related promotion, on your web site.

♦ **Know your audience's promotional preferences.** Some consumers love coupons, sales, and discounts. Others don't. If you're not sure of your audience's promotional preferences, use a survey, a poll, or a choice of interest list to sort your subscribers into groups.

5. Confusion and Illusion

Sometimes consumers report legitimate email as spam because they simply want to get off a list and don't understand the negative impact of hitting that spam button. Here are two reasons why consumers might choose the spam button over the more forgiving option of unsubscribing.

♦ **Your subscribers can't figure out how to unsubscribe.** If your audience has trouble finding the unsubscribe link at the bottom of your email, use a permission reminder at the top of your email that includes the link.

♦ **Your subscribers don't trust the unsubscribe link in your email.** Use your sign-up process and welcome email to reinforce the ability to safely unsubscribe from your list by clicking the unsubscribe link in any of your emails.

While it may be impossible to take the sting out of receiving a spam complaint, it is possible to minimize the amount of complaints you receive. Stick to permission-based tactics, make your identity clear, send relevant content, and keep tabs on your frequency. If you put all these tips into practice, then you've done everything in your power to keep subscribers on your list and stop them from clicking the spam button when they receive your emails.

Adhering to the CAN-SPAM Act

There are laws protecting consumers from all kinds of corrupt business practices, and spam is no exception. While this law will not stop spam, it does make most spam illegal and ultimately less attractive to spammers. The law is specific about requirements to send commercial email and empowers the federal government to enforce the law. The penalties can include a substantive fine and/or imprisonment for up to five years. The law also includes a private right of action clause for Internet Service Providers (but not for individuals) to sue a sender regarding the receipt of prohibited messages.

While I am not an attorney and therefore cannot provide legal advice, I feel it is important to provide you with Constant Contact's interpretation of how the federal law may affect you. This is a summary of some provisions of the law and is not a full analysis of how it may apply to you. If you believe you may be affected, you should consult with your own attorney.

The CAN-SPAM (Controlling the Assault of Non-Solicited Pornography and Marketing) Act went into effect January 1, 2004, and it preempts all state laws. This means it overrides all individual state spam laws (39 at last count). The great news is that now you only have to comply with one law—the federal law.

If you use an Email Service Provider such as Constant Contact, you are already in compliance with much of the federal law, but there are a few other things you need to know. Constant Contact's terms and conditions require that your list is permission-based, which means that you already comply with the unsolicited email requirements stated in the law:

 ♦ Your email header information is not misleading because it is set for you by Constant Contact.

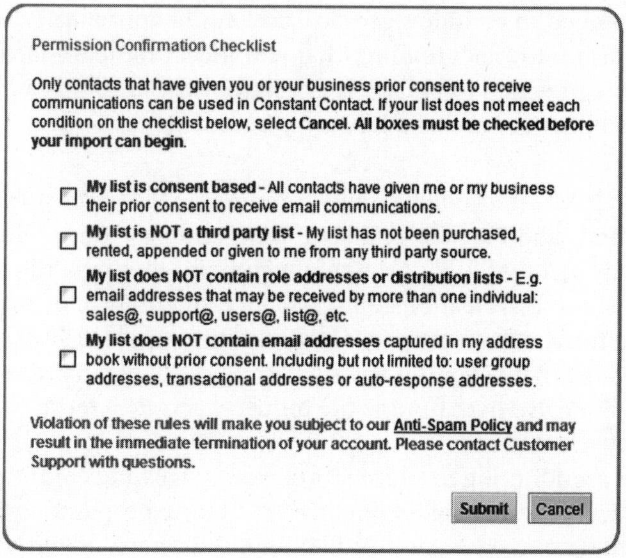

Permission Confirmation Checklist

Only contacts that have given you or your business prior consent to receive communications can be used in Constant Contact. If your list does not meet each condition on the checklist below, select **Cancel**. **All boxes must be checked before your import can begin.**

☐ **My list is consent based** - All contacts have given me or my business their prior consent to receive email communications.

☐ **My list is NOT a third party list** - My list has not been purchased, rented, appended or given to me from any third party source.

☐ **My list does NOT contain role addresses or distribution lists** - E.g. email addresses that may be received by more than one individual: sales@, support@, users@, list@, etc.

☐ **My list does NOT contain email addresses** captured in my address book without prior consent. Including but not limited to: user group addresses, transactional addresses or auto-response addresses.

Violation of these rules will make you subject to our <u>**Anti-Spam Policy**</u> and may result in the immediate termination of your account. Please contact Customer Support with questions.

[Submit] [Cancel]

Figure 4.3 Using Constant Contact helps keep your emails compliant.

- Your email's From address is verified and already accurately identifies you as the sender.

- Constant Contact automatically includes the ability for your contacts to opt-out of future email communications.

- Constant Contact automatically processes unsubscribes from your email communications.

Constant Contact even asks our customers to confirm the lists they upload comply with our policy as shown in Figure 4.3.

Even if you use an Email Service Provider that helps keep you in compliance, there are a few more things you need to be aware of going forward.

- Make sure that your email campaign's "Subject" line is straightforward, not misleading. The days of using cute phrases or tricks to boost open rates are over. The recent Adteractive settlement reinforces the FTC's commitment to enforce this requirement.

- If you aren't already doing so, any unsubscribe requests that come to you via a reply to your email must be honored within ten days of the request.

♦ You need to include a physical address in your email campaigns. Constant Contact requires that you add a physical address before you can schedule a campaign: make sure that this address is a valid physical postal address for your organization.

In May 2008, the Federal Trade Commission (FTC) released its Statement of Basis and Purpose and Final Discretionary Rule ("Final Rule") on the CAN-SPAM ACT. This statement contains four new rules and also contains some clarifications and guidance to the text of the original act in the form of the Statement of Basis and Purpose (SBP).

Note also that since the rules are new, it's likely that the interpretations will evolve over time as the industry acquires more experience with implementations.

If you are adhering to your ESP's current terms and conditions, making sure that your messages contain a valid company name and physical address, and not working with affiliates or third-party advertisers, there are probably only a few things you need to consider:

♦ You should review the From address and From name you are using in your emails. At least one and preferably both of these should be clearly recognizable as belonging to your organization.

♦ Make sure you are not "procuring" the forwarding of your campaigns by offering any kind of incentive (e.g., coupons, discounts, T-shirts) to your recipients. Forwarded messages that contain incentives to forward will be noncompliant under CAN-SPAM because they will be considered commercial messages and will not contain the required opt-out mechanism.

♦ There were some modifications to the definition of "sender" in order to clarify the required CAN-SPAM compliance when there are multiple advertisers in a single message. In general, it clarifies that the From address visible to your recipients should be clearly recognizable as belonging to your organization. In addition, if you work with affiliates or you have third-party advertisements in your email campaigns, you should review the new rule provisions relating to the definition of sender as it relates to multi-sender emails.

♦ The opt-out mechanism must not be complicated: "an email recipient cannot be required to pay a fee, provide information other than his or her email address and opt-out preferences, or take any steps other than sending a reply email message or visiting a single Internet web page to opt out of receiving future email from a sender." (The Constant Contact opt-out mechanism is compliant with the new guidelines.)

♦ Commercial mailers may now use a valid P.O. box as the required physical postal address in their messages, as long as it is valid and meets USPS registration guidelines.

♦ The term "person" has been defined as "an individual, group, unincorporated association, limited or general partnership, corporation, or other business entity." This is intended to clarify that CAN-SPAM's obligations are not limited to natural persons.

If you are a single organization sending email on your own behalf and do not publish ads from third parties in your emails, then the new rules will likely have little impact on you unless your opt-outs do not comply with the new stricter opt-out guidelines.

If you work with a third party (other than Constant Contact) that manages your opt-outs for you, you should consult with that company to make sure that its mechanism will comply with the new rule provisions.

The Final Rule also provides some additional guidance, the Statement of Basis and Purpose, on aspects of the Act that it does not explicitly cover. Although these items are not officially mandated, they give guidance on how the FTC is likely to interpret applicability and compliance, and in that context should be given careful consideration.

♦ The FTC clarifies that forward-to-a-friend mechanisms, which have generally been treated as exempt from CAN-SPAM because they are one-to-one messages from the original recipient to a friend, may in fact be subject to CAN-SPAM if the originator of the message "procures" the forwarding or if the forwarded message is stored in any way by the forwarding system.
  ○ A message has been "procured" if "the seller offers money, coupons, discounts, awards, additional entries in a sweepstakes, or the like in exchange for forwarding a message."

  ○ Because most forward-to-a-friend mechanisms are not set up to include opt-out links that would make the message CAN-SPAM compliant and enable the final recipient to opt-out of future messages from the original sender, this means that any forwarded message whose forwarding has been "procured" would make the original sender noncompliant under CAN-SPAM.

o To ensure you're not caught by this clarification, you should make sure that you're not offering any incentives in the content of your email campaigns that encourage your recipients to forward them. For example, "forward to 10 friends and get a 10% off coupon," or "get a free T-shirt" would likely classify your forwarded message as commercial and thus, subject to CAN-SPAM.

♦ There is fairly extensive guidance given on the definition of a "transactional or relationship message." The FTC decided not to exempt entire classes of messages from CAN-SPAM, but rather requires they be considered on "a case-by-case basis depending on the specific content and context of such messages." If all of your communications are already CAN-SPAM-compliant, then you don't need to worry about these clarifications; if you do treat some of your communication as transactional, you probably want to look at this section in more detail to ensure that you're not impacted by the clarifications.

♦ The FTC has decided not to alter the time limit (10 days) for honoring an opt-out request. In addition, it reaffirms that there is no time-out on an opt-out request, i.e., that it may only be overridden by a subsequent explicit opt-in request.

To read the federal law, you can visit www.ftc.gov/os/caselist/ 0723041/canspam.pdf.

How Four Types of Permission Can Make or Break Your Strategy

The CAN-SPAM Act was created to provide the federal government with the ability to pursue blatant spammers. The requirements under the Act should be considered the minimum standards for legitimate senders of email campaigns. As email marketers we are not just trying to comply with the law, we are also trying to build our reputation, trust, and loyalty with our recipients.

In order to deliver beyond the requirements of the Act, you need to practice permission. Overdeliver on the expectations you set and strive to enhance your relationship with each communication you send.

The following sections explain the four types of permission and give you some rules to follow so you can impress your customers and build trust.

NO PERMISSION

Sending emails with no permission is a violation of the law, but the worst thing that can happen to your business when you send permissionless emails doesn't have anything to do with federal fines. You'll get spam complaints. Lots of them.

Spam complaints are your recipients' way of telling you that, for one reason or another, they no longer want to hear from you. In the case of some email programs (AOL, for example), they actively tell their customers to use the "This is spam" button rather than unsubscribe. When people receive an email they didn't ask for, they are much more likely to report it as spam. A spam complaint is your recipient's way of telling you that he has lost trust in you.

It's also important for you to keep in mind that permission has to be renewed by your recipient in some cases. Sometimes consumers react negatively to email after a certain event has occurred. For example, the bridal industry is notorious for this. While a bride-to-be is willing to hear from one and all about weddings and bride-related topics leading up to her wedding, the day after the wedding she seems to have an adverse reaction to receiving those communications. Accordingly, wedding caterers, photographers, bands, and the like are subject to having a time-sensitive audience.

I suggest that industries with time sensitivity put their recipients into list groupings by the month of the event and then delete the lists or ask for permission again as each month passes.

IMPLIED PERMISSION

In this form of permission, a relationship exists between you and the recipient that implies he will know who you are when you send an email communication. This may be because the recipient has been a customer of yours for a number of years or maybe he attended an event at your place of business.

I could just say that if your recipient doesn't know who you are, then you don't have permission. However, this is an area of confusion to some people, so let's look at it a little deeper.

There are instances where it is crystal clear that you don't have permission. For example, if someone were to offer you an opportunity to buy an email list, this is clearly a situation where you do not have permission. The recipients on a purchased list have no clue who you are, and if you send to this list, you and your business will be labeled as spammers.

Other areas of permission are a little less clear. Let's say you join a local Chamber of Commerce and notice that as a member you have access to the membership directory that includes email addresses for all the members. You crawl the directory and create a list of the members to send an email marketing campaign to since you, too, are now a member. Ask yourself, do these people know you? No. In fact, you may have violated one of the provisions under the CAN-SPAM Act, which prohibits crawling web pages for email addresses. No matter how you slice it, do NOT send an email campaign to people who don't know you.

That does not mean you can't engage them in a one-to-one email dialogue by going through the list and sending an introduction to each member letting him or her know that you just joined the Chamber. In fact, you could use this introductory email to tell them about your monthly newsletter and even include a link in your email that points them to where they can sign up for your list. However, you cannot send a bulk email campaign to the group. That is spam.

Email appending is another gray area. We at Constant Contact do not believe this is a legitimate way to build a list. Others have differing opinions, but we believe if the recipient has not provided you with his or her email address, then you don't have permission and you should not send. Email appending uses known email formats to come up with potential email addresses for individuals on a list. For example, you know my name is Eric Groves and you know I work at Constant Contact. The companies that provide email–appending services will provide you with a list of potential email addresses when you provide this basic information. In my case, they would provide you with ericg@constantcontact.com, egroves@constantcontact.com, eric@constantcontact.com and so on. At the end of the day, if you are sending me a message and I don't know who you are or how I ended up on your list, there is no trust or relationship. I am just going to delete it and worse, if you call, your reputation with me is below where it would be if you just called.

As you can tell, the potential for the recipient to react favorably or not to your communication depends greatly on the relationship and the level of trust in that relationship.

If you aren't sure if you have the right kind of permission, I recommend that you use a permission reminder at the top of your emails when sending to a list that includes greater than 30 percent implicit permission email addresses. A permission reminder is simply a text message at the top of your communication that informs recipients why they are receiving your message and includes an unsubscribe link to make it easy for your recipient to remove themselves from your list if they do not want to continue receiving it. Constant Contact allows you to turn this on or off in every email with a toggle button in the product.

It is perfectly fine to include email subscribers with implied permission on your email list. However, it is important to recognize that you need to take the aforementioned additional steps to ensure your communications continue the process of building trust.

EXPLICIT PERMISSION

This highly recommended form of permission is attained when the recipient explicitly signs up to receive email communications from you. This typically takes place either on your web site through a signup box or by signing up in person by adding his or her name and email address to your customer email mailing list.

The key element in both of these situations is that the recipient is actually signing up directly for your email communications and is looking forward to receiving them from you.

It is important to remind your new recipient that she has been added to your list. For example, Constant Contact provides an automated welcome email that is sent automatically after someone signs up. If you are collecting the addresses either at point-of-sale or via an online form, it's a good idea to set up an initial email that confirms that people have been added to your list.

CONFIRMED PERMISSION

Confirmed permission is actually a form of explicit permission that requires the individual being added to your list to go through an

Figure 4.4   Confirmed permission requires clicking an additional link after signing up.

additional email confirmation process. When someone signs up, he receives an email that requires him to click on a link in the email in order to be added to your list—even though he may have already explicitly signed up. (See Figure 4.4.) Once the recipient clicks on the confirmation link, he is added to your list. If he doesn't click the link, the subscriber isn't added to the list.

This process is recommended for businesses that are either dealing with government agencies, security professionals, or have an audience that has a high concentration of technology professionals. These groups tend to require a double-opt-in process and are therefore used to the added step required.

This added step in obtaining Explicit Permission is not required for most businesses and organizations. In fact, in most cases where it is used with an audience that is not used to the process, the added step causes a loss of more than 60 percent of the individuals that sign up for your list due to the confusion caused by the added step in the process.

If you decide to go with confirmed permission, you'll gain higher loyalty and probably better delivery, but you'll lose some subscribers who either don't understand the process or aren't willing to click the link.

For more information and the latest trends in permission-based email marketing, check out Constant Contact's Learning Center and our *Hints & Tips* email newsletter. Permission is a hot topic, and we're always writing about how you can take advantage of the best practices in permission.

5

Building a Quality Email List

I recently ate dinner at Bobby Flay's Bar Americana restaurant in New York City. I expected dinner to be great. In fact, it was excellent. Following dinner, I used the comment card provided by the restaurant to tell them how much I enjoyed dinner. When I returned to my office in Waltham, Massachusetts, I found an email waiting for me from Tyler, the restaurant manager. The email thanked me for my comments and invited me to contact him in the future if I ever needed assistance in getting a reservation at any one of their restaurants.

I would probably have returned to a Bobby Flay restaurant just because of the experience, but this simple outreach by Tyler extended my experience well beyond my time at the table. Now I'm excited for my next visit, because I have a new connection at a famous restaurant. It even makes me want to share my good experience with the thousands of people reading this book. Not bad for a first connection!

There's a great lesson here. If a restaurant chain with fame, fortune, and success still finds the time to make ongoing connections with its customers, every business should find the time to do the same.

This chapter shows you how to build a quality customer email list by identifying your customer connection points, determining which points provide the best opportunity to make a connection, and showing you how to make a connection that enables you to easily build and grow your list.

Finding Places to Make Valuable Connections

What makes my Bobby Flay experience different from my experience with most other businesses is that Bar Americana leveraged my great experience into a connection. Most businesses don't take advantage of the multitude of opportunities they have to leverage the experiences they create. Instead, most businesses leave future connections to chance and hope that someone will return after a first touch. Accordingly, this results in the whole experience ending soon after the customer walks out the door. Most of the time extending an experience and making a connection is as simple as collecting contact information at every touch point.

Your email marketing list is the engine that powers your ability to connect with your customers, build lasting relationships, and ultimately build trust. In short, it is a critical business asset.

Finding the sources of your most valuable future customers requires a little investigative work on your part. In the following sections, I'll explain what makes a valuable connection and show you where to find them. Some are obvious, others are elusive, all are critical to your success.

I enjoy meeting people, so every time I connect with someone it's valuable to me. It's crucial, however, to recognize the difference between making connections that are valuable to you and making connections that are valuable to your business.

You probably already know that you need to get your message in front of a lot of people to attract enough customers to stay in business. But collecting email addresses from everywhere and everyone doesn't spell success unless it results in value to your business. If you're meeting with or communicating to a lot of people, you need to learn to recognize the value opportunities so you can focus on them and avoid spending time collecting information that won't result in value.

What differentiates a "connection" from a "valuable connection" is simply whether you have the ability to continue the dialog beyond the initial connection in a way that is likely to result in sales. Here are some questions you should ask yourself to determine whether you should spend time collecting information. If you can answer "'yes" to all of the following questions, it's a valuable connection.

1. Is the contact information valid and direct to the decision maker? Don't collect email addresses such as sales@abccompany.com or webmaster@abccompany.com. Those email addresses are too generic and aren't likely to result in a personal connection.

2. Is the person you're collecting the information from interested in what your business offers? Some businesses insist that everyone is a prospect, but this simply isn't true. If your target doesn't have financial means, is already loyal to someone else, or just made a similar purchase and seems reluctant, don't waste your time. There are plenty of opportunities to collect from interested prospects.

3. Is the place where you're collecting the information conducive to establishing a relationship? For example, being confronted with the decision to sign up for a financial planner's email list during a trip to the bank is more likely to be perceived positively than being confronted with the same decision during dinner at a restaurant with the family. Therefore, placing an email sign-up list or guest book on the counter at all the banks in town will result in a more valuable connection for the financial planner than placing a sign-up card at all the restaurants in town.

Mapping Out Your Connection Points

The first step in creating valuable connections is identification of your best sources for new customers. With these in hand you can then trace the touch points your customers have with you and ensure you are set up to collect the information that enables you to continue the dialog.

Contrary to what you might believe about privacy and personal sensitivity, most people will provide their email address to your business if you ask politely and demonstrate value in being on the list. If you have not set yourself up to ask for their information, then you are letting a huge business asset walk away.

In many cases it costs significant amounts of money to generate new connections. You might be missing opportunities to recoup your investment if you aren't asking for contact information from every connection at every touch point. Some of these connections may buy from you immediately, others may take time to cultivate, and some may never buy from you but may refer you to others. All of these connections are more valuable for your business if you have the ability to maintain contact.

Where do you interact with customers and prospects?

☐ Retail storefront
☐ Web site
☐ Local networking events
☐ Tradeshows, conferences, industry events
☐ Phone
☐ Email

Figure 5.1   Possible sources of customer connections

Take some time to write down all the possible sources of customer connections. Figure 5.1 offers a few suggestions (If you would like to download this table along with the rest of Constant Contact's Email Marketing Workbook go to: www.constantcontact.com/workbook)

These include all the ways you interact with people and every touch point within each source. The following sections provide some examples of sources and touch points you can use as a reference for realizing your own.

It should go without saying that your sources and touch points need to be legal, ethical, and in line with consumer preferences. You can read more about these issues in Chapter 4.

INTERNET SOURCES

Hopefully you connect with people on your web site's home page, but people visit all kinds of online sources including

♦ all the pages on your web site

♦ your blog

♦ social networking pages

♦ online directory listings

♦ natural search listings on search engines

♦ web sites that offer maps and directions to businesses

♦ paid search listings

These online sources typically result in people who join your email list on the web site itself, but these sources might also prompt an inbound phone call, personal visit, or email inquiry, so it's important to map out these sources and touch points as well.

PERSONAL CONTACT SOURCES

Face-to-face interactions and one-to-one conversations represent great opportunities to engage individuals in an interesting dialog and collect information. These touch points include

- inbound phone calls
- walk-ins
- networking events
- tradeshows
- speaking engagements
- social events

REFERRAL SOURCES

Once you have mapped out the most obvious connection points, make note of the sources where others might help you accomplish your goals by referring someone else to join your email list. These touch points include

- current customers
- family and friends
- the media
- colleagues
- business partners
- suppliers or account reps

People are more likely to refer others to your email list if being on your email list is valuable enough to share with others. If you want more referrals, I don't recommend paying people to collect emails for you or offering financial incentives in exchange for growing your list. Instead, ask your referral sources to refer people they know who are going to appreciate the value of the email list. That way, your referral sources won't be tempted to find unqualified leads for you, and your referrals will value your emails instead of joining your email list just to be nice or to help their friends.

EMPLOYEES

If you have employees interacting directly with customers, it's important to share with them the importance of making connections and collecting contact information. A brainstorming session with your employees is a great way to solicit innovative ideas, connect with your employees, and have them engaged in the ongoing process.

You may also want to set up a rewards program that recognizes the employees who are most successful in making great customer connections.

NETWORKS

There are networks of people everywhere who have a vested interest in seeing you succeed. Since one of the best ways to help you succeed is helping you to build your email list, ask the network or organization leadership to assist you and the other members. For example, if you're a member of a business association or chamber of commerce, ask other association members if they will assist you by collecting email addresses and permission from people who call the organization seeking information about the products and services their members offer. You could also ask them to facilitate a members-only email address exchange program so all members have an opportunity to subscribe to valuable information available from other members.

Tips for Maximizing Email Address Collection

Mapping out your sources and touch points is a great first step toward recognizing all the opportunities you have to build your email list. Once you have a handle on the scope of your strategy, you can apply the tactics in the following sections to start collecting as many permission-based email addresses as possible.

COLLECTING ON WEB SITES

The web sites I frequent are most often those of small businesses and organizations. It never ceases to amaze me that so few of these web sites contain a way for the visitor to actually connect with the web site owner.

Figure 5.2   Use your ESP to create a sign-up link or form on your
web site.

A business web site is a major connection point and should be
thought of as a place to demonstrate your value along with an offer to
visitors to stay connected over time. Adding a "Join My Mailing List"
(JMML) link or sign-up box on your web site makes it easy for visitors
to add themselves to your email list.

Your web site programmer can create a JMML link, or you can easily
create one through your Email Service Provider as shown in Figure 5.2.
Constant Contact allows you to create and customize your own JMML
link and generates the HTML code so all you have to do is copy it and
paste it into your web site.

When you're creating and customizing your link, it's better to avoid
using the generic "Join My Email List" call to action as your only link
or headline. Instead, include a brief but compelling message about the
value of subscribing, along with a link to a privacy statement. Here are
some helpful tips on how to make a JMML sign-up experience easy
and engaging for your visitors, and a more effective marketing tool for
you.

1. **Get your subscribers to self-correct.** When people sign up
   for your list, they may misspell their email address without realizing it. Have them confirm their email address by typing it twice
   before they are added to your list. Otherwise, the emails you
   send them will end up as a bounce—a lost opportunity for both
   you and them.

2. **Only ask for what you can use.** While it may be tempting to know lots of fascinating facts about your new subscribers, most people don't want to spend more than a few seconds filling out a form. So, keep it short and sweet. Only ask for information that helps you send relevant and targeted communications. Requiring just "first name" and "email address" will get you the highest number of subscribers. You will also have numerous additional opportunities to collect information in the future.

3. **Tell them what you're sending.** Are you sending a monthly newsletter or weekly coupons? Do they contain articles, promotions, event invitations, or all three? You can answer these questions by providing a one- or two-sentence description of your email content in a link or on your sign-up form.

Since you are not physically involved in the interaction taking place during a web site sign-up process, you'll need to find other ways to make the experience more personal.

One way is to provide a link to an archive of past email campaigns. This enables your visitors to view information that you have shared with your valued connections in the past before asking them to join your email list. You can read more about creating and utilizing email archives in Chapter 14.

Customer testimonials can also be used in this fashion to demonstrate the value of your email list before asking someone to join. Just have your customers share their insights into what makes your email list unique and ask their permission to post their comments near your JMML link.

You'll also get more traction on your JMML links when you make them prominent on every web page and include a strong call to action. Don't hide your JMML link on the "Contact us" page of your web site. It needs to be prominently displayed on every page for people to find it and sign up for your list. Find a prominent location on your web site near the top of the screen, and place your JMML link in the same spot on every page in your web site. That way, visitors don't have to scroll to see the JMML link, and they can see the link no matter which pages they visit on your site.

Including something of value encourages more people to sign up for your list, but you need to choose what you offer very carefully to avoid attracting an audience that isn't really interested in receiving your information. For example, a financial planner should offer a certificate for a free 60-minute consultation for anyone who signs up rather than a chance to win a trip to Disneyworld. That way he or she can be more certain that the people signing up for the list are interested in meeting a financial planner and not just meeting Mickey Mouse.

SOCIAL MEDIA AND BLOG SITES

Your own web site isn't the only web presence that can host your JMML link. If social media web sites such as Facebook, Myspace, or LinkedIn are also important touch points for your business, place your JMML link on these sites as well as your own web site.

To invite your Facebook or MySpace friends to join your email list, you can add a JMML link by copying and pasting the HTML generated by your Email Service Provider in much the same way as you copy and paste the HTML to add it to your own web site.

Some social media sites don't allow you to add complex HTML code. In these cases, you can simply create a link to your email list sign-up form or register a domain name or URL such as "JoinMyEmail-List.com" or "mycompany.com/email-list" and place the URL on the page as text or a link.

IN EMAILS

How many emails do you send and reply to every day? Each one represents a touch point and an opportunity to make a connection. Your email signature is a convenient place to allow people to join your list without compromising the intent of your one-to-one emails. See Figure 5.3 as an example.

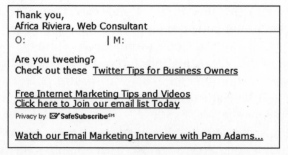

Figure 5.3   Place a sign-up link in your email signature.

Email programs don't read form fields, so you won't be able to copy and paste a JMML box. However, you can include a link to your sign-up page, privacy statement, and images in most email signatures. Check the help files in your individual email program for instructions on pasting HTML or links into your email signature.

It's also a good idea to place a JMML link or box it in your email newsletters, promotions, and other marketing emails. Why would you bother to include a JMML link in an email that gets sent to the people who are already on your email list? Because emails are often forwarded to friends and those friends represent touch points who can join your email list.

Also, if you archive your emails to your web site—and you're using an Email Service Provider like Constant Contact who has enabled this function—the forward link on the archived email still works. This means people who visit your email archive page on your web site can forward information to their friends and colleagues as if the email was still in their inbox. You can read more about email archives in Chapter 14.

INBOUND EMAILS, MOBILE PHONES, AND LAND LINES

If inbound email requests are one of your business's touch-points, ask the people you respond to if they would like to join an email list related to the topic they are emailing you about. Remember that just because someone sends you an email, it does not equate to permission to add him or her to your marketing email list. Instead, ask for that during the course of responding to the inquiry.

Inbound phone calls also provide a great opportunity to engage with a prospective customer and gather his or her contact information. Be sure to have a sign-up form near every phone to remind you and your employees to ask callers if they would like to be added to your email list. A great way to ask callers for their information when they ask a question is to answer the question and then let them know that you answer all kinds of similar questions in your monthly email newsletter. Then ask the callers if they might have an interest in receiving ongoing communications related to their question.

Mobile phones present a unique opportunity to ask for email addresses as well. Asking voice callers to join your email list is one way to do it, but people also use text messaging and email on mobile phones in increasing numbers. If your customers are on the go, ask them to join by texting their email address to your mobile number or by sending an email with "Join the Email List" in the subject or body of the email.

Networking

Networking events are a great way to build an email list because they involve personal interaction. When you swap business cards at these events, take several seconds to write down on the back of each card what you talked about and whether the person is interested in receiving your marketing emails. Immediately following the event, send a follow-up email to all who were interested to thank them and remind them that they will be receiving your valuable emails going forward.

Networking also provides opportunities for partnering with other businesses or organizations. Think of a business or organization you have met that is related to your business, but not a competitor. You can work together to promote each other"s email lists to your customers. Some good partnership examples are a tax accountant and a financial planner, a public relations firm and a web site designer, or a theater and a nearby restaurant.

At the Counter or in the Office

Walk-ins require little effort to make a great impression. The individual is already partially invested in learning what you have to offer by walking in your door. Now it is up to you to reward her investment by stopping what you are doing and engaging her in conversation. While I am not suggesting that you should put on the hard sell from the moment someone walks in the door, simply engaging customers and letting them know you have a valuable email list is enough to start the conversation flowing.

Placing a sign-up list on your desk or checkout point is a great way to ask for email addresses. It's also effective to have a sample of your best marketing email printed out and displayed next to your sign-up list so people can see the value and start to recognize your branding.

Tradeshows and Events

Tradeshows represent another personal touch point, but remember that quality is more important that quantity when it comes to these events. I have seen many businesses ruin their email lists by adding email addresses provided by tradeshow organizers instead of adding only the email addresses belonging to people with whom they made a connection. Many attendees at tradeshows stop by your booth to see what free gifts they can obtain for their office or kids. These are not the people you want added to your email list.

I recommend separating all collected business cards into two piles. The first pile are people who asked for more information about your business. They're expecting you to follow up. Go ahead and email them your Welcome Letter and attach a copy of your last email newsletter or a related promotion. Then, show them what they'll receive in future mailings and give them an easy way to subscribe or unsubscribe if they prefer not to be on your list.

The second pile is for people with whom you had social contact but didn't fully engage. They didn't ask for, nor do they expect, any follow-up. Those are the ones you need to ask permission to send them your email newsletters or promotions. You can send those people a personal email asking for their explicit permission to be added to your mailing list, but don't automatically add them just because you have their business cards. Remind them about the event where you met, asking if they would like to subscribe to your emailing list. Tell them how subscribing will benefit them. If they sign up, great! If they don't, cross them off your list and cut your losses there.

HARNESS TRADITIONAL MARKETING TOOLS

Any form of traditional marketing is an opportunity for email list growth, if you find yourself making connections through them. You can advertise your email list in print advertising, television ads, radio ads, and outdoor advertising. Use a portion of your ads or create entire campaigns to describe the benefits of signing up, and then give a web site address that points to your sign-up form. If you produce brochures, white papers, articles, or other communications that highlight your organization in print form, make sure to include a plug for your email list so you can send the same communications electronically in the future.

When it comes to building an email list, you should always think about quality versus quantity. However, if you take the time to evaluate all of your touch points and train yourself and your employees to properly collect a prospect's email address and permission, you will be amazed at how fast your list will grow.

6

Making Your Email List More Valuable

Imagine two music stores for sale on the same street. Both music stores have lots of guitars, keyboards, drum sets, and other instruments. They both offer lessons, repairs, and a friendly staff. They both have convenient parking, good signage, and lots of drive-by traffic. Both stores have the same square footage and both are listed for sale at the same price.

The value of these two music stores might seem the same when you examine their physical assets, but one store is actually worth much more than the asking price while the other represents a significant risk to the buyer. Here's why.

The store that represents a risk to the buyer relies on drive-by traffic, time-consuming phone calls, and expensive print advertising to attract new and existing customers to its in-store promotions and its web site.

The more valuable store gains new customers the same way as the risky store, but the staff has also worked hard to collect email addresses and permission from the thousands of musicians, parents, and music teachers who have visited the store over the years. As a result, this store has been able to continually attract customers to the store and the web site at a very low cost by emailing promotions, event invitations, and holiday sale announcements. It also continually adds more personalized information to its email list in order to remember birthdays, follow up on recent purchases, and send promotions that are targeted to the exact instruments its customers play.

Whether you're buying a business, starting a business, or running a business, it's important to know how much money the business is making, but it's even more important to know how reliably and cost-effectively you can continue to generate sales for your business into the future.

If you have an email list, that's a great first step toward decreasing your costs and increasing the value of your business, because you've obtained a low-cost way to contact your customers and bring them in to make purchases. Your email list is even more valuable to your business, however, when you continually capture additional information such as interests, personal information, and corrections. Your email list is also made more valuable when you take measures to increase reliability, familiarity, and regularity.

This chapter provides ideas on how to continually improve the value of your email list, which will, in turn, add more value to your business and your ability to predictably sustain and grow your revenue.

Strike While the Iron Is Hot

When someone is in the process of signing up for your email list, his or her interest and curiosity are at high points. People who are interested in your business will share information, but they aren't going to give you unlimited time or get too personal. Their interest is also likely to decrease quickly if you wait too long to send your first email, if you send irrelevant information, or if you send too much or too little information in the first few days or weeks following sign-up. This represents two challenges.

The first challenge is to determine what information is valuable to your business, how much information you need to collect in order to communicate effectively, and how much information your new email list subscriber is willing to share at the beginning of a new relationship.

Your other challenge is to begin communicating in highly relevant ways within a short period of time so your new email list subscribers remain interested and start getting used to seeing and interacting with your emails.

The next sections show you which and how much information you should be asking for as a starting point and how to make sure your first few emails are effectively set up to collect additional information and maximize the interest in your business following an initial signup.

VALIDATING EMAIL ADDRESSES

Email addresses can be quite unusual, and as a result they are prone to being mistyped, misspelled, and juxtaposed when someone enters them into a database or email sign-up form.

To minimize mistakes, make sure your online sign-up forms require your subscribers to enter their email addresses twice for verification at sign-up, as shown in Figure 6.1. This simple step, while it requires the same information to be entered twice, validates a match, and virtually eliminates typographical mistakes.

If you have a retail store or an office and you use a guest book to collect email addresses, make sure you ask your prospects and customers to print legibly and use block letters. If you collect email addresses when exchanging business cards with people, make sure you ask everyone whether the email address on the card is the best place to send your marketing emails. Some company email addresses are subject to more filtering and blocking than personal addresses, and your new subscriber is probably just as willing to share either email address.

When you enter email addresses into your database, make sure you use a program that validates correct email address formats so

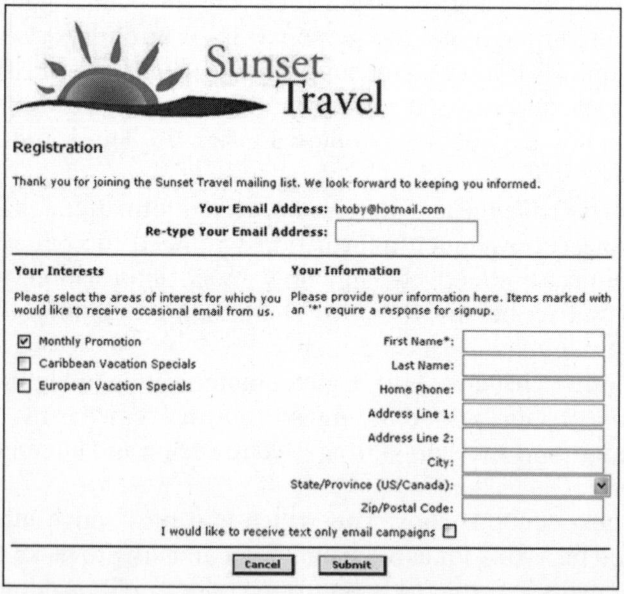

Figure 6.1   Ask your subscribers to enter their email address twice.

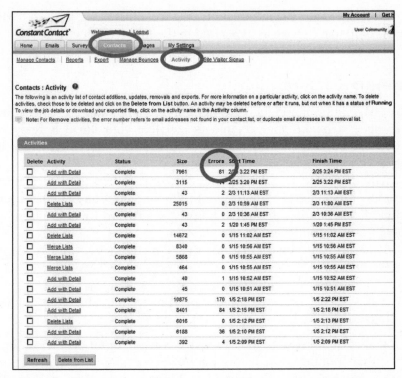

Figure 6.2   Make sure you check for errors when uploading email addresses to a database.

you can make corrections. For example, Constant Contact generates a list activity report every time one of our customers uploads an email list (see Figure 6.2). The report checks each email address to make sure it has an @ sign and a familiar extension such as .com, .net, or .org.

COLLECTING PERSONAL AND INTEREST INFORMATION

In addition to collecting a valid email address, you should collect information that allows you to personalize your emails and target specific interests.

Generally speaking, the less personal information you ask for when someone first signs up for your email list, the more people you'll convince to complete the sign-up process. However, it's also important to ensure you have enough information to send meaningful and relevant information to people and to position yourself to ask for more in-depth information as your relationship gains trust.

Create a list of the information that you must have, need to have, and would like to have as explained in the following sections.

Must-Have Information

Must-have information includes the minimum amount of information you need to make your recipients feel like your email is relevant and personal to them. Must-have information should be required, as opposed to optional, for every subscriber.

The challenge for your business is to make sure the information isn't too personal and to minimize the amount of required information while demonstrating that providing the information will bring more value to the subscription.

Here are the non-negotiables that I recommend you ask every subscriber for.

- ◆ First name. That way you can personalize the salutations in your emails.

- ◆ Special interest. If your audience is made up of distinct groups that require special information. For example, a music store should identify guitar players and drummers so they aren't sending drum set promotions to the guitar players.

- ◆ Geography. If you're sending event invitations to people in multiple areas who aren't willing to travel, or if you have a need to send promotions related to a specific business location.

Need-to-Have Information

Need-to-have information isn't critical to initial relevancy and success, but it's critical to collect soon so it's available at strategic points in the future. For example, a phone number isn't required to send your first few emails to a new subscriber, but it sure comes in handy when an email address bounces back and you need to get in touch with the customer to obtain a new email address.

The necessary data fields vary significantly from business to business, but the key to success isn't necessarily in nailing the exact data. It's more important to set up your programs to collect additional information at relevant points over the course of your entire strategy.

You can start to collect need-to-have information at sign-up by making some of the fields on your email list sign-up form optional. The more information you request from your subscribers, the greater the likelihood they will abandon the sign-up process. The general rule we've used at Constant Contact is that you can typically ask a subscriber to provide up to four additional non-required items in addition to his or her email address before he or she starts to abandon the process.

The other way to collect need-to-have information is to collect it in the future during the normal course of executing your email strategy. You can use surveys, polls, and links in your emails to ask for additional information, and there's no limit to how much information you can ask for, as long as your questions are relevant to the context of your communications and don't get too personal too soon.

You'll probably be more successful if you ask for personal interest information than if you ask for personal demographic or behavioral information. Need-to-have personal interest information typically includes data used to target emails to a particular audience, and people are often willing to share interests when they understand that it will result in more relevant information.

For example, a travel agency may service travelers interested in family and singles destinations. Clearly, in most cases a subscriber would be interested in one but not both of these destination types. You could ask for that information at sign-up but some people might not want to get that personal at first. So, you could send a survey asking which types of vacations your new subscribers enjoy, or, by providing both options in an initial email promotion to a new subscriber, you can find out his interest when he clicks one or the other of the two options, and you view the click on your email tracking report.

In this case, if the travel agent were to send the same communications to everyone and the first several communications were all about family vacations, then you run the risk of having your singles destination audience tuned out to your communications when you eventually send out a singles destination alert.

Nice-to-Have Information

Nice-to-have information includes anything that helps you in running your business but does not necessarily help build a relationship with the recipient. An example of this type of information is to understand how the recipient found your web site. Rather than include a request for this information as part of your signup process, I recommend including this as a one-question survey in your welcome email or your first auto-responder message. I tell you about those email formats in the following sections.

SENDING WELCOME EMAILS

When someone signs up for your email list, sending a welcome email within the first 24 hours gives you the opportunity to make a first impression, deliver important information, suggest an initial response to the subscription, and begin the process of building brand identity.

Constant Contact sends a welcome email automatically when someone subscribes to one of our customer's email communications through its web site visitor sign-up form. Other Email Service Providers include similar functionality in their applications. Sending a welcome email is statistically proven to improve the responses to your first few email messages, because your subscribers are more likely to recognize them and remember signing up for your list (see Figure 6.3). Here are some tips on how to make the most of this communication:

   1. **Tell them what to expect.** Your sign-up form doesn't tell subscribers much about what they will receive from you. Sell them

Figure 6.3   Your welcome email makes an important first impression.

on the value of being a member of your list by highlighting the content—from great events to money-saving discounts—your future emails will include.

2. **Reward them instantly.** Subscribers are at the height of their interest when they sign up for your list. Validate the wisdom of their decision to subscribe with an "instant reward." If your emails are educational, provide links to past articles or past issues that you have on your web site. If your emails are promotional, offer a discount or an incentive to encourage them to take immediate advantage of what you have to offer. Restaurants do a great job with this. I've gotten many "welcome" emails that include a coupon for 20 percent off or a free appetizer. If I wasn't planning on going there for dinner that week, I am now!

3. **Lead them back to the web site.** You've worked hard to make your web site a great place for visitors to get information. Make sure your welcome email links them back to helpful information on your site that might interest a prospective or new customer.

4. **Look professional.** This is your first email communication, and it sets the recipient's expectations for the quality of what you will be delivering in the future, so make the most of it. Make sure to customize the look to reflect the colors, branding, and personality of your business.

5. **Personalize your message.** Have the message come from you or someone significant within your business. An initial email coming from info@yourcompany.com doesn't have the same personal impact as yourname@yourcompany.com.

6. **Encourage outreach.** Provide the recipients with a way to contact you directly with any questions they might have. Remember, you are trying to establish a relationship, so the more information you can provide (email address, direct phone, after hours contact, etc) to the recipients that enables them to connect with you, the better.

7. **Include something of value.** Thank your subscribers by including a coupon for something of value that can be redeemed by their taking the next step in building a relationship. This could be as simple as a free 60-minute consultation or 20 percent off their first visit to your store.

8. **Include a link to a survey or a poll.** Let your subscribers share additional information about themselves and make their experience more relevant and personal.

USING SUBSCRIPTION AUTO-RESPONDERS

Auto-responders are preset email communications that are triggered by an event or the passage of a specified amount of time after an event—such as the moment a subscriber joins your email list. Auto-responders allow you to continue the dialog beyond your welcome email without the need to manually create or schedule email communications every time you get a new subscriber. Auto-responder emails allow you to:

♦ Introduce new contacts to basic information about your organization over the course of several emails.

♦ Address newcomers' frequently asked questions.

♦ Remind contacts of your new relationship between your welcome email and your first periodic email.

♦ Save time and avoid missing an opportunity to communicate with a new subscriber if you get busy and let too much time lapse between sign-up and an initial email.

While the welcome email is sent immediately and automatically in most situations, auto-responders can be sent a day, week, or even several weeks after a subscriber has joined your list. Here are three tips for setting up an auto-responder:

1. **Keep your messages short.** Each auto-responder message should include one major point that you are trying to convey along with one call to action.

2. **Don't overdo it.** Just because you can send a message every day does not mean that you should. Try spreading out your messages over several weeks.

3. **Three is enough.** If you are sending regular email communications to your list, then three auto-responder messages should suffice to keep the communication process moving forward until your next email newsletter.

Here is an example of an auto-responder flow for a day spa business:

1. **Auto-responder 1.** Delivered one day after joining list. Topic: A stretch to relieve lower back pain. Call to action: link to single question survey on how you found us.

2. **Auto-responder 2.** Delivered seven days after joining list. Topic: Two pressure points that ease headaches. Call to action: link to web site where you can find other pressure points and what they relieve.

3. **Auto-responder 3.** Delivered fourteen days after joining list. Topic: Why it's important to drink water after a massage. Call to action: link to web site where you can get 30 percent off your first massage. New customers only.

As you can see from this flow of communications, it was not until the third and final auto-responder communication that we actually mentioned anything about scheduling services at the spa. After that communication, it's time to start sending more spontaneous and targeted emails.

Auto-responders are great time savers, but they can also feel impersonal or generic if you don't hold to some best practices. They also have the potential to result in overcommunicating to your audience if you don't schedule them appropriately. Here are some best practices and tips to keep in mind when creating and scheduling auto-responder emails.

♦ **Keep the content timeless.** The whole point of creating auto-responders is that you can set them up and let them run without the need to make frequent changes to the content. Avoid putting references to dates, holidays, upcoming events, and seasons in text or photos.

♦ **Do not refer to other emails.** Although it is okay to create your auto-responder emails as a "series," where the content in each consecutive email may build on and complement one another, don't label auto-responder emails with issue numbers or refer to other emails. You can't assume that each new contact receives or reads all of your auto-responder emails. For example, if you schedule a new auto-responder email to be sent one *week* after a contact signs up and another new one to be sent one *month* after signup, all contacts who have been on your email list for more than one week, but less than one month will only receive the second auto-responder email. As a result, the second email cannot refer to the first email because these contacts will not receive the first email.

♦ **Provide answers to frequently asked questions.** Since new contacts are the only ones who receive auto-responder emails, keep their interests and questions in mind when planning and creating them. Explain what resources are available on your web site and introduce key people in your organization.

♦ **Reuse well-regarded articles and information.** Use auto-responder emails as an opportunity to share information that your existing subscribers have already seen with your new contacts.

♦ **Create content for new contacts to save.** Sending information that your customers and prospects need to refer to more than once and asking them to save it is a great way to make your auto-responder emails live beyond the inbox. Include your company's contact information, your subscriber's account information, links to your web site, policies and instructions, maps, catalogs, or anything your audience might need on an ongoing basis.

♦ **Collect feedback and information from newcomers.** To gather feedback from just your new contacts, send a survey invitation email with an auto-responder. You may want to ask new contacts where they first heard about your organization, why they are interested in you, where and when they made their last purchase, or what products and services interest them the most.

♦ **Collect information about new contacts.** After a new subscriber has received your welcome email or several of your standard emails, he is more likely to be willing to share personal information he wasn't willing to share at initial signup. You can schedule an auto-responder email to ask contacts for personal information after several weeks or even months after sign-up without the need to keep track of the exact date every one of your individual subscribers joined your list.

Increasing the Value of a List over Time

As time passes, your emails present an opportunity to ask for increasing amounts of information with more depth and meaning. It's also necessary to keep up with changes in your email list and apply corrections when necessary.

The following sections offer suggestions for adding in-depth information to your subscriber information through surveys and polls, keeping your information current with subscription reminders, and protecting your data from problems with good list management practices.

GATHERING ONGOING FEEDBACK THROUGH SURVEYS AND POLLS

Email communications are all about you speaking to your customers. However, in any relationship listening is equally important (some would argue more important) as speaking. The best way to listen to your customers is to set yourself up to get a constant flow of customer feedback. It's called "drip intelligence," and it gives you customer feedback on a regular basis. If you ask the right questions, the feedback you'll get will be easily actionable, timely, and will give you a leg up against your competition.

It's simple to do. Simply include one customer feedback question in every email newsletter you send. Here is how it might work.

If you're publishing a quarterly email newsletter, insert a link to one of these questions in each newsletter. If your email newsletter goes out monthly, do the same thing, and then start the cycle over again the fifth month, repeating each of the four questions in sequence. Compare your results to the first communication and track your results over time.

- Month 1: Your customer's perception of the products/services you provide.

- Month 2: Your customer's perception of your approachability.

- Month 3: Your customer's propensity to tell others about you (see Figure 6.4).

- Month 4: How you can provide even better service.

- Month 5: Start over again at Month 1.

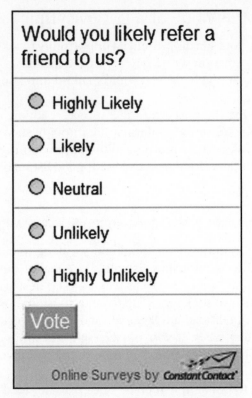

Figure 6.4   Polls help you read trends in your customer base.

It's important to thank respondents for their participation. Send a special email to all of the people who answered the survey, thanking them for taking the time to share their thoughts with you.

Share your survey results. Once you've made business adjustments based on what you learned from your survey question, report those changes back to your customers in your next communication. Let them know you're not only listening but you're acting based on what customers want and need. And let them know how other survey respondents who shared their concerns answered the question.

Write smarter, better newsletter content. It also goes back to something we coach our customers on every day: Writing really good content that speaks to their customers' wants and needs. The more you know about your customers and their interests, the more you can tailor the content of your email marketing communications to hit on the topics of most importance to them at that point in time.

By getting feedback, you not only gain critical information to help you adapt quickly to changes in customers' perceptions about your business, but you also can stay one step ahead of your competition.

The closer you are to your customers—the more you're seeking their feedback and answering their questions—the more likely they are to turn to you when they need the products or services you offer. Customers will see you as someone they have a relationship with—someone who cares about their needs, appreciates their hardships, and wants to know what they think.

Sending Subscription Reminders

Permission is perishable, so it's important to try and stay connected to your audience. One way to do this is to do a quarterly, semiannual, or annual permission reminder mailing to customers on your list who have not opened a communication for a long time.

This communication should be very short and should contain a subject line that informs the recipient that action is required to stay on your list. The communication should include a simple link that requests the subscriber click on the link if she would like to continue to receive communications from you. Then keep those who click on the link in your database while moving those that don't click out of your list. If recipients have not opened your campaigns in a year and do not click on this link, then they don't care about what you are sending and for all intents and purposes have unsubscribed.

Protecting Your List: Don't Share/Sell It or You'll Violate Trust

It's important to protect all of your critical business assets, and that goes for your email list as well. Protecting your list means not only keeping it within a secure database, but also limiting access to your account and never sharing your list with others.

Securing Your List

Have you ever received an email communication where the list of recipients is in the "To" or "CC" line of the email? When a sender uses his email client (like "Outlook") to send email messages to a large number of recipients, he runs the risk of his list being obtained by others.

Email Service Providers like Constant Contact send email messages to only one recipient at a time, eliminating this concern.

Another way to protect your list is to limit access to your email account. In the event that an employee leaves who had access to your account, then immediately change the password to your account. If you allow third parties to manage your account, be sure to have a legal agreement that prohibits them from doing anything other than your communications with your list.

As your lists grows in value to your business, it will also grow in value to others wanting to reach a similar audience. Never give, sell, or lend your list to another business. It's OK for you to cross-market another business or organization within your communications. In fact, having another business promote you to its list and vice versa is a great way to mutually expand your spheres of influence. Remember that your customers have entrusted you with their email addresses. It's your responsibility to protect that trust.

7

The Three Rules of Valuable Email Content

Writing great content is often identified as a major obstacle to email marketing. Coming up with great content keeps your email list subscribers opening your emails and responding in greater numbers. If your content isn't up to par, subscriber boredom can set in and unsubscribe requests increase.

Creating great content can be challenging, but it doesn't have to be daunting. Great content is a matter of having a well-thought-out strategy, the right perspective, a list of reliable sources, and attention to volume.

This chapter helps you to create valuable content by showing you four rules to follow. This chapter also shows you examples of real small businesses who create valuable email content on an ongoing basis. These Constant Contact customers are models worth following because they have demonstrated that success can be achieved in a variety of different industries and approaches.

Use these rules and examples as a guide to create your own email content and your email marketing is likely to keep your subscribers engaged, your emails appreciated, and your sales in a state of healthy growth.

Rule 1: Work Off a Plan

Have you ever been in a relationship with someone who could not stop talking about himself or herself? You may tolerate self-centered chatter in short doses out of politeness, but over time it's exhausting, and it usually drives people apart. If your email content is all about you, your subscribers are going to have the same reaction.

Now contrast that to a friend who pays attention to your interests, gives you valuable feedback and advice, and looks forward to hearing from you as much as you look forward to hearing from him or her. Each interaction with such a friend leaves you feeling energized and looking forward to the next interaction.

When you create your email content, it's important to work off a plan so you make sure your email content has the characteristics that your customers want before you say what you need to say to reach your goals.

The most important email content characteristics are explained in the following sections. When you are sure that your plan addresses these characteristics, the content you create or draw from is more likely to have these characteristics too.

PAY ATTENTION TO CUSTOMER INTERESTS

Don't assume you know what your customers want to hear about. It's a great idea to formally ask your customers what they want to hear about through online surveys, polls, and link tracking, but you can also make some educated guesses based on what you notice about your prospects and customers.

The following are questions we use at Constant Contact to help us gather our thoughts and create content when we don't have formal feedback to rely on. Take out a piece of paper and answer the questions below. Think about how you might use them to create relevant content.

These questions are contained within the Constant Contact's Email Marketing Workbook. To download it, visit: www.constant contact.com/workbook.

1. What are the top five questions that your customers ask?

2. What articles have you read recently that your customers might find interesting?

3. Who are the most interesting customers that you helped in the last six months?

4. What might make them interesting to other customers?

5. What problems do you foresee your customers encountering this year?

6. What can you do to solve these problems for them?

7. What information do your customers need to make better decisions about your products or services?

Another way to make sure your content is valuable to subscribers is to give them some influence over what topics you cover. Simply add a question-and-answer section to your email newsletters or email promotions, conduct an ongoing survey focused on content, or simply ask for reader feedback in every email. Giving your audience opportunities to be heard and even seen—such as highlighting their names and businesses along with their questions—makes their experience more personal and helps you to forge a deeper connection with them. You can also ask them for feedback on the products you offer so that you can decide which ones to promote.

Figure 7.1 shows a simple one-question survey that Mom 4 Life (www.mom4life.com) used to collect information from its readers on the value of a specific product. This survey provides Mom 4 Life with great feedback on not only the product but also the likelihood of purchase. This information can be used by the company to identify potential customers, determine appropriate inventory levels, and to search for other products with even greater potential based on the feedback provided.

Give Valuable Feedback and Advice

When your customers, clients, or members think of your business or organization, what words do you want to come to their minds? Are you knowledgeable? Available? Professional? Reliable? Email content is a reflection of your brand, and your brand has to be consistent. Your email content also has to have value apart from the value of your product or service offerings, because your email content has to keep people interested when they receive your email and aren't ready to buy. That way, they'll look forward to receiving every email, not just the ones they receive at the moment they are thinking about making a purchase.

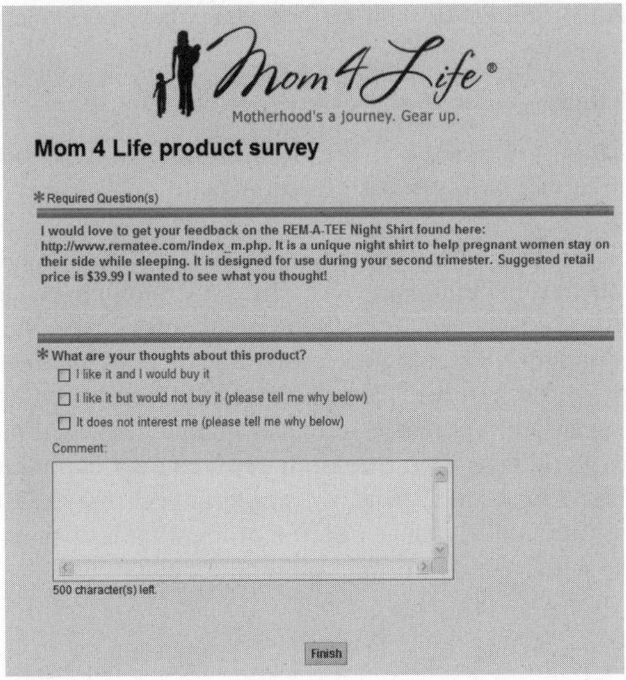
Mom 4 Life®
Motherhood's a journey. Gear up.

Mom 4 Life product survey

* Required Question(s)

I would love to get your feedback on the REM-A-TEE Night Shirt found here: http://www.rematee.com/index_m.php. It is a unique night shirt to help pregnant women stay on their side while sleeping. It is designed for use during your second trimester. Suggested retail price is $39.99 I wanted to see what you thought!

* What are your thoughts about this product?

- I like it and I would buy it
- I like it but would not buy it (please tell me why below)
- It does not interest me (please tell me why below)

Comment:

500 character(s) left.

Finish

Figure 7.1 Mom 4 Life uses email surveys to ask about new products and content.

A good starting place after you understand what your subscribers love about your current content is to figure out how you can help them in their daily lives. Email content that helps to solve a problem is always welcome. Even if you don't think of yourself as an expert, your customers probably turn to you because of your expertise. Think about ways that you can share more of that expertise with them over time.

> Bob Corlett, President of Staffing Advisors (www.staffingadvisors.com) prides himself on collecting and delivering content to his readers that they need but don't have the time or resources to find. Bob believes that when you offer your readers something of value, they will come to you when they are ready. He takes great pride in keeping anything "sales-y" away from his content.

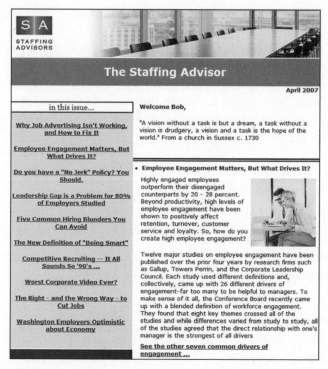

Figure 7.2   Staffing Advisors gives practical advice.

As he puts it, "I share the best thinking and research I can find and include links to white papers and other resources. If someone agrees with my viewpoint, he typically gives me a call." Bob is a great example of how to turn the sharing of knowledge into revenue-generating business.

Look Forward to Hearing from Your Customers

In order to tell if your content is valuable to your audience, you have to listen as much as you speak. Don't assume that your customers are interested in everything you send out. For example, not all consumers respond to discounts, coupons, and other types of financial savings. Some of your customers might want to stay up to date on the latest and most expensive products available instead. A lot of consumers care more about quality or making an informed decision than just saving money.

Part of your email content plan should involve keeping track of the responses you get from your email content so you can make changes to your plan when your assumptions aren't correct or when the interests in your audience change (such as during a recession). You can tell whether your content is effective because email is capable of so many responses, including:

♦ Replies to your emails. Don't just read them, keep track of them and watch for trends.

♦ Clicks on links. If you get a lot of clicks on a particular topic, make a note so you can include that topic in future emails.

♦ Unsubscribe requests. If you get a lot of unsubscribe requests, it could be a sign of content that isn't working.

♦ Forwards. When people forward your emails, they are telling you that your content was valuable enough to share.

♦ Surveys and polls. If your feedback isn't clear, send a survey and ask more questions.

Keep track of each and every response and all your feedback so you can continue to improve your content and in so doing gain more trust and loyalty.

You can learn a great deal about your customers through their actions when your email arrives in their inbox. Blind Lemon Vintage (www.blindlemonvintage.co.uk) in Figure 7.3 is able to identify each of its readers who clicks on the "discounts offer" link in the above campaign. This information can then be used to segment Blind Lemon Vintage's list and deliver specific offers and campaigns to customers it knows to be motivated by discounts.

Rule 2: It's Not About You

Let's face it. If you have done a good job of making a connection that resulted in your collecting a prospective customer's email address,

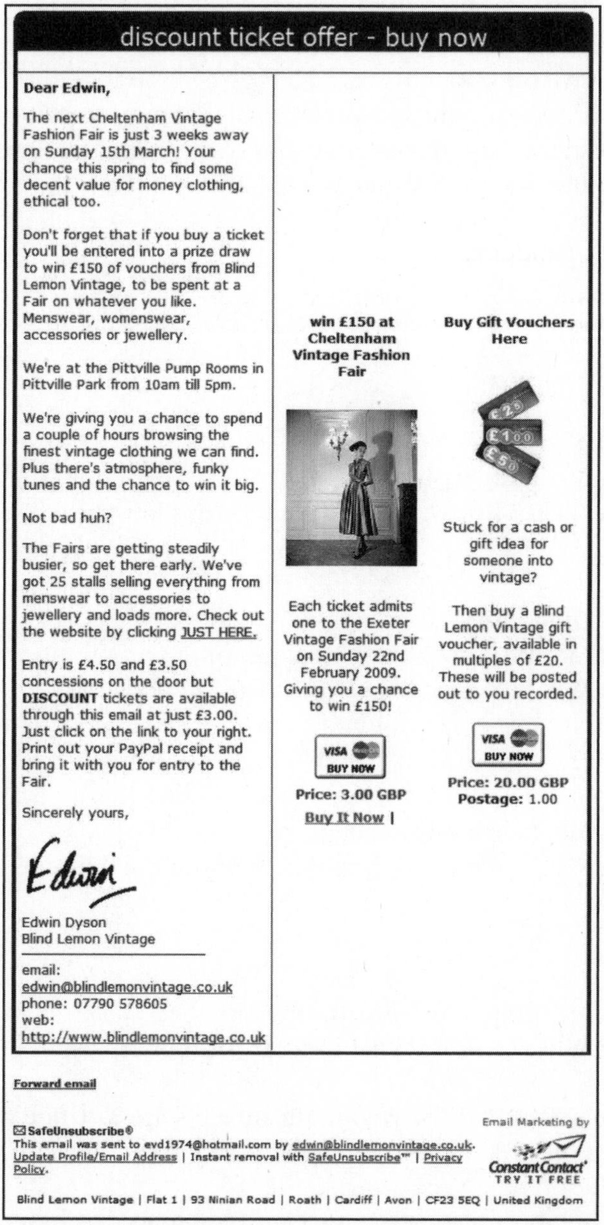

discount ticket offer - buy now

Dear Edwin,

The next Cheltenham Vintage Fashion Fair is just 3 weeks away on Sunday 15th March! Your chance this spring to find some decent value for money clothing, ethical too.

Don't forget that if you buy a ticket you'll be entered into a prize draw to win £150 of vouchers from Blind Lemon Vintage, to be spent at a Fair on whatever you like. Menswear, womenswear, accessories or jewellery.

We're at the Pittville Pump Rooms in Pittville Park from 10am till 5pm.

We're giving you a chance to spend a couple of hours browsing the finest vintage clothing we can find. Plus there's atmosphere, funky tunes and the chance to win it big.

Not bad huh?

The Fairs are getting steadily busier, so get there early. We've got 25 stalls selling everything from menswear to accessories to jewellery and loads more. Check out the website by clicking JUST HERE.

Entry is £4.50 and £3.50 concessions on the door but **DISCOUNT** tickets are available through this email at just £3.00. Just click on the link to your right. Print out your PayPal receipt and bring it with you for entry to the Fair.

Sincerely yours,

Edwin

Edwin Dyson
Blind Lemon Vintage

email:
edwin@blindlemonvintage.co.uk
phone: 07790 578605
web:
http://www.blindlemonvintage.co.uk

win £150 at Cheltenham Vintage Fashion Fair

Each ticket admits one to the Exeter Vintage Fashion Fair on Sunday 22nd February 2009. Giving you a chance to win £150!

VISA BUY NOW

Price: 3.00 GBP

Buy It Now |

Buy Gift Vouchers Here

£20 £100 £50

Stuck for a cash or gift idea for someone into vintage?

Then buy a Blind Lemon Vintage gift voucher, available in multiples of £20. These will be posted out to you recorded.

VISA BUY NOW

Price: 20.00 GBP
Postage: 1.00

Forward email

SafeUnsubscribe®
This email was sent to evd1974@hotmail.com by edwin@blindlemonvintage.co.uk.
Update Profile/Email Address | Instant removal with SafeUnsubscribe™ | Privacy Policy.

Email Marketing by Constant Contact TRY IT FREE

Blind Lemon Vintage | Flat 1 | 93 Ninian Road | Roath | Cardiff | Avon | CF23 5EQ | United Kingdom

Figure 7.3 Blind Lemon Vintage is able to track customers who click on discount offers.

then that customer already knows what you have to offer. Email marketing provides your audience with the rationale for making you the one they turn to for it!

What is it about you and your business that makes you different? This is what you want to convey in your email messages. Here are some industries and potential About Me and About What I Know topics:

Landscaping Company
About Me: 20 percent off de-thatching
About What I Know: Three plants deer won't eat

Day Spa
About Me: Free wash with cut
About What I Know: How to stretch your lower back

Financial Adviser
About Me: Monthly Newsletter, August
About What I Know: Three tips to get an IRS audit

Nonprofit
About Me: Donations needed
About What I Know: Community helps to build house

Retail
About Me: 20 percent off all suits
About What I Know: What to wear to an interview

You may feel that the About Me subjects are just fine and in fact they might result in a desired response. However, they are just good, not great!

Good subjects resonate with your recipients but have the effect of ending their distribution at the recipient (not getting forwarded). They also have the potential to reduce trust over time. For example, in the fall of 2008, how many times were you bombarded by a big box retail store offering you an ever-increasing discount if you bought from it during its desperation to sell by year-end? It was ridiculous. I was getting daily emails with 20 percent, then 40 percent, then 70 percent off offers. Did this make me want to buy from these companies? No, in fact, I unsubscribed from their email lists.

Great subjects resonate with your recipients, engage them, educate them, make them want to do business with you, and have the added benefit of being shared with others. If you share great insights with your audience, they will reward you by sharing your ideas and your business with others. It's human nature. We all want to look smart to our friends, so when we learn something we share it. Great email marketing is rewarded with increased trust over time.

One of my favorite email newsletter writers is Michael Katz (www.bluepenguindevelopment.com). Michael teaches businesses large and small how to write great email newsletters, and his monthly newsletter is something that I very much look forward to reading. In fact, I have given it the ultimate in email recognition—its own folder in my inbox. Michael's email newsletters are captivating because he takes everyday occurrences and turns them into insightful ideas on how to write better email content. In short, Michael uses his everyday experiences to help his audience become better writers. Michael does not need to tell you that he is available to help you write your content because you already know that. Rather, by sharing his knowledge with the readers, he helps make us all better writers. It's pretty clever because at the end of the day, if we recognize the value of great writing and the impact it can have on generating business, we are likely to turn to Michael if we need help. Clearly Michael has a knack for writing engaging content. You may think this is beyond your abilities, but it's not. You don't have to go overboard with humor but do make your stories come to life.

Rule 3: Choose a Variety of Sources for Your Content

Now that you have a good foundation of a plan, the next sections uncover the tactics for finding and creating great content. I encourage

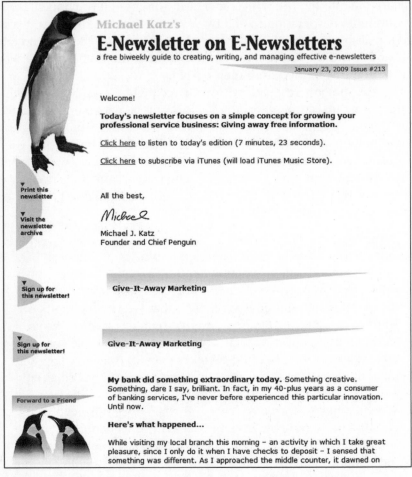

Figure 7.4   Blue Penguin Development has a unique personality.

you to take a manila folder and label it "content ideas." Keep this folder on your desk, and when you come across a great idea for content, put it in the folder. It's a lot easier to write great content when you have a folder full of ideas to turn to.

The following are some ideas we've seen our most successful customers use at Constant Contact. Some of them are easy to find or create yourself. Others are more challenging. All of them have been tested and proven successful by businesses of all types.

BE AN EXPERT

If you own a business, you're an expert. At least, that's what your customers believe. Even if you don't think of yourself as a leading authority, you certainly know more about your business than your customers do. Use your newsletter as a platform to solidify your expert status by providing credible advice and information.

Share your knowledge with your customers. The easiest topics to write about are the ones that you know well. Because you live and breathe your business, you have insights and information that your customers don't. Build your credibility by providing advice on timely issues that can help them in their daily lives. For example, a company that sells motorcycles might give its readers advice about riding in the wintertime, while a tax accountant may include tips for preparing taxes in January.

Justify purchase decisions for your customers. Your customers don't have time to keep up with all the reasons to buy what you are selling. When you know about products and services that could be a great fit for them, tell them why. Write an expert article about the benefits of the services or products you have available. For example, a web designer who also offers search engine optimization (SEO) could write about how web site activity and online sales increase when SEO is implemented.

So how do you get great content ideas from your customers? Remember the old adage that if one person asks you an interesting question, then odds are ten other people are wondering the same thing. So when someone asks you an interesting question, write it down and put it in your folder. Simply answering customer questions can make for a really engaging newsletter.

If you are going to use this approach, you might also want to consider involving your customers even more in the process. By creating a "Stump Me" section of your newsletter, you can ask your readers to submit questions for you to answer. You can reward the question of the month with something special along with recognition in your newsletter on whose question you picked.

Michael Bartus of Home Twin Cities (www.hometwincities. com) does a great job of engaging his readers by including a simple

Figure 7.5   Home Twin Cities uses questions to gain reader participation.

one-question survey within his email campaigns. The question not only captures your attention by asking you some trivia regarding the area that Michael covers with his real estate business, but he also offers a prize for the first person to get the right answer. In addition to engaging his audience, this approach also helps build Michael's reputation as a local knowledge expert, which is one of the keys for success as a real estate agent.

RELY ON YOUR CUSTOMERS' EXPERTISE

Another option is to make your customers the experts. Sometimes they have a simplified perspective, and they often value things about your products and services that you aren't aware of.

Let your customers give advice. Instead of giving subscribers your tips, ask a few of your best customers what advice they would give other customers. For example, a gardening center might send an email newsletter with customer tips and ideas for creating indoor gardens. The gardening newsletter could include related offers for plants mentioned in the newsletter.

Be an expert interviewer. Interview your customers about their experience or expertise and share the interviews with your audience. For example, a travel agent might interview a customer who recently took a trip to one of its featured destinations. In this case, including a few photos from the customer's trip would be a great addition.

Jodie Turner of Lucky Duck Web Design (www.luckyduckweb design.com) uses her email newsletter to showcase her most recent customers and their stories (see Figure 7.6). By enlisting her customers' input into her communications, she allows them to sing her praises while benefiting her customers by driving traffic to their websites. Traffic to her clients' web sites works out great for Jodie as well, since visitors see Jodie's creations in action.

TELL A STORY

There's nothing more powerful than an authentic customer testimonial. While collecting and sharing quotes from customers who have great experiences with your business is always a good idea, try including the following types of testimonial content in your emails for a fresh change.

- ◆ **"Felt and Feels" articles.** When writing an article about a customer experience, use the "Felt and Feels" approach. For example, an online jewelry retailer could offer a new engagement ring in the context of a story about a customer who Felt nervous about buying a discounted engagement ring online and now Feels that he made the right decision because of the quality, the buying experience, and the positive response from his new fiancée.

- ◆ **In their own words.** Ask some of your most satisfied customers if they would write a brief story (a few paragraphs) about an experience they had with you or one of your employees. For example, a hardware store customer might write about a home

Figure 7.6   Lucky's news and views features customer testimonials.

project that went awry and the difference the advice of an in-store expert made.

♦ **Writing customer case studies.** Customer case studies are stories that demonstrate a challenge, a solution, and a result. They are fun for your customers to read and can help you to further convince readers of your expertise or their need of what you offer. Start with the challenge your customer was facing (she needed to lose weight for a wedding), then the solution (a friend referred her to a weight loss program), and end with the results (she lost 30 pounds in six months and had fun doing it).

Flexperience (www.flexperienceconsulting.com) is a unique consulting agency. By connecting seasoned industry experts who are interested in part-time or flexible work schedules with companies looking for additional bench strength, it is able to create a win-win situation for its consultants and clients. By highlighting one of its consultants' stories in each of its communications, it is able to keep its content fresh and engaging while continually demonstrating the depth and talent available within its organization (see Figure 7.7).

USING OTHER PEOPLE'S CONTENT

Another great source for content is referencing content written by others. Whether you are a landscaping company or a financial analyst, you come across information in your area of expertise that your average customer would never uncover. Accordingly, when you find an article that does a particularly good job of explaining something of interest to your audience, merely sharing this content can reinforce your value to the recipient. I would like to point out that it is *NOT* OK to simply lift someone else's content as your own. If you are going to quote or reference someone else's work, it is important to get permission and give the source proper attribution. If you come across a great article like that, print it out and put it into your manila folder. Be sure to note the source and author's contact information so that you can track him or her down for permission to use the work.

LOCAL CONNECTIONS

Another way to come up with engaging content is to connect with another business owner in a related industry and to write content together. For example, a restaurateur and a wine store owner could team together and create a monthly communication that pairs interesting wines with great recipes. As an added touch, you could feature those wines and recipes for that month at your respective businesses, and as Emeril would say "Bam!" You have some great content that has

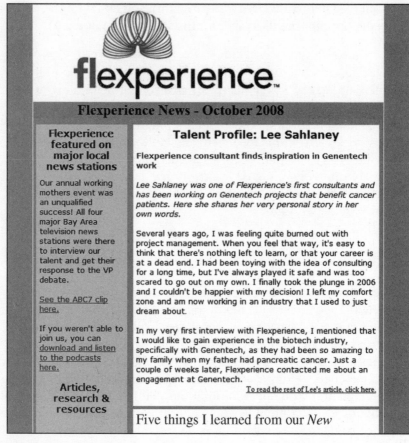

Figure 7.7   Flexperience uses personal stories to reinforce its value proposition.

the added benefit of driving traffic to your business. Other connections that could be made:

1. A book store and a financial adviser where the financial adviser creates fun games for kids to understand saving and investing. The book store can then host quarterly coffee hours with the adviser where kids are invited to act out these games while the parents grab a cup of coffee and wander around the book store.

2. A nonprofit that collects coats for kids can connect with a retail store; for each coat collected, the person making the donation

receives mention in the retail store's Keep Someone Warm email newsletter.

3. A Chamber of Commerce can leverage its members for Advice from Our Local Members section of its communications and solicit business owners for their suggestions. This is a great way to deliver value back to your members, engage the local business community by making connections, and focus local businesses on buying products and services from each other.

Writing content may seem difficult on the surface, but every day you experience things that would make great content for your readers. It's often hard to remember these ideas when you sit down to write, so try to add a topic or two per week to your content folder and you will always have a great supply at hand.

8

Creating Email Content That Leads to Action

Whether your email content is designed to inform, promote, or relate, it has to capture attention and provide paths that your customers and prospects can take to move them closer to a decision or purchase. These paths might involve getting in touch with you, learning more about a product or service, or buying what you offer.

Without leading your subscribers down these paths, your emails are prone to being deleted without much meaningful or measurable interaction. Mapping out the various paths and actions that you want your recipients to take when they read your email content helps you to create and organize your email content for the greatest impact. Content that's organized around a path to action also helps your subscribers better understand what your emails are asking them to do.

There are multiple types of email content, and there are often multiple paths to action in a single email. This chapter explains how to come up with a variety of different types of effective email content and offers advice on using content to call your subscribers to action. I also give you tips for coming up with sound objectives, organizing your email content, and making sure your objectives and content lead to action. I also explain how to insert different types of links into your emails using your Email Service Provider to aid your recipients in taking action quickly and easily.

Tying Email Content to Your Objectives

Before you create an email, you should set a primary objective that governs your content decisions. This objective helps you set the tone of your email content and helps you avoid mixing messages or targeting the wrong audience. An objective also helps you in giving your audience what they want so you can balance the needs of your audience with the need to push your own agenda.

For example, Constant Contact sends out a monthly email newsletter called Email Hints & Tips. While the email highlights our services and provides a path for referrals, the primary objective for Email Hints & Tips is to educate our customers on email marketing best practices so they can be more successful using our products. Even though we have hundreds of thousands of subscribers who are not yet our customers, we are careful not to insert overwhelming calls to action focused on selling our products or services. Instead, most of the calls to action involve links to full-length articles that are summarized in the newsletter, links to customer support options, and links to tutorials or webinars covering the newsletter's topics in more detail.

We do this because we know that the noncustomers who subscribe to Email Hints & Tips aren't interested in signing up for Constant Contact immediately. If they were, they would have signed up to receive information about product features or discounts. We know that more of the noncustomers on the list are going to become customers if we respect the fact that they are interested in learning some best practices before signing up for the product. Selling to them before they are ready just drives them away and fails to make a valuable connection or build trust in the relationship.

The next sections explain the steps to defining your objectives and paths to action so you can create content that meets the needs of your audience while accomplishing your objectives.

DEFINING YOUR PRIMARY OBJECTIVE

Your primary objective does not have to be your only objective, it just needs to be the main focus of your email content each time you send. If your email content doesn't have a chance of meeting your objectives, it's not worth spending the time to create it.

To determine this objective, ask yourself what you want your email to accomplish when it lands in the recipient's inbox. Use the following three main objectives as a guide.

- ◆ Promote
  - ○ Motivate purchases: Drive traffic to your web site or store, an affiliate program, make an appointment. . .

  - ○ Increase event attendance: Register online, RSVP, buy tickets, invite a friend. . .

- ◆ Inform
  - ○ Inform potential customers: New products, customer support, share expertise. . .

  - ○ Differentiate my business: Describe features and benefits, customer testimonials, industry facts. . .

- ◆ Relate
  - ○ Increase loyalty: Special invitations, press releases, greetings, and thank-you cards. . .

  - ○ Encourage more referrals: Rewards programs, forward valuable information, invite a friend to an event . . .

DEFINING YOUR AUDIENCE'S MAIN INTEREST

Your email content has to accomplish your goals, but it also has to be valuable to your audience. Not all people respond to discounts, coupons, and other types of financial savings. A lot of consumers care more about quality or making an informed decision. You can figure out what motivates your customers and prospects by using surveys, talking with them in person, and by watching your email tracking reports to see what offers they respond to.

Once you have a sense of what your audience is interested in, use these categories to determine which type of email content can meet both your needs and the needs of your audience.

If your audience is most interested in saving money:
- ◆ Send promotional email. Include content that pertains to a valuable offer.

If your audience is most interested in making an informed decision:

♦ Send informative emails. Include content that is inherently valuable.

If your audience is most interested in product quality:

♦ Send relational emails. Include content that makes them feel special.

You might find that you have more than one type of interest group on your email list. If so, divide your list into different groups so you can send the appropriate content to each group. For example, you might want to send a coupon to the people who value savings and a testimonial to the people who value quality.

I also recommend that you provide the members of your email list with offers and information related to your products and services that are not available to the average walk-in customer. They have provided you with something of value—their email address—so provide them something of value in return.

BALANCING MULTIPLE OBJECTIVES

In certain circumstances, you will want your email content to accomplish more than one objective. For example, a garden center whose primary objective is to educate its customers about choosing the right plants might also want to hold a promotional event related to choosing a plant. Combining objectives can be effective as long as you follow these three rules:

1. **Use the 80/20 rule if your main objective is to inform.** Informative content should represent 80 percent of your message with the promotional content representing no more than 20 percent.

2. **Group your content into categories.** Place promotional content in one section of the email, such as a column or box, so it's visually distinct from your informative content.

3. **Tie multiple objectives together with a theme.** For example, if the aforementioned garden center is promoting indoor plants, the event should be related to indoor plants.

I often find it interesting when people write really long emails and put a coupon at the very bottom. There's nothing wrong with that if your primary objective is to inform, and the coupon is related to your informative content. However, if your primary objective is to get lots of people to use the coupon, don't bury it at the bottom of a long email newsletter. Instead, feature the coupon by placing it closer to the top and keep your informative content short and to the point. Here are some tips for including coupons in emails with multiple objectives:

1. Make it stand out if your primary objective is to promote.

2. Make it special. Remind your recipient that the offer you are providing is being made available solely to the people on your email list.

3. Tie it to your audience's interests. Remember, not everyone is interested in a discount. Use coupons to offer special privileges or exclusive trials to satisfy the need for quality or making informed decisions.

Promotional emails and coupons are most effective after your business has built trust with your subscribers. Otherwise, promotional emails can be trust-busters. If your business survives on offering discounts and special offers, make sure you set your subscribers' expectations when they sign up for your email list so that your promotional messages are welcome. If you send promotions to an audience that is more interested in quality or information, your promotions will result in your audience becoming less interested in your messages. It may not happen overnight; however, it will happen.

Writing Great Email Content

Coming up with email content on an ongoing basis can be challenging, especially when time is a factor. The execution of an excellent email content strategy relies heavily on the effectiveness of the content you write. If you are the person writing for your email campaigns, it would be wise to invest some time into strengthening your skills.

Good copy helps your readers understand what you are offering them and gives them clear ideas on how you want them to respond. The following sections show you Constant Contact's best copywriting tips and email content sources. Keeping these tips and sources in front of you when you write helps you to create compelling content that engages your readers.

CHOOSE AN AUDIENCE

Before writing your first word of copy, you need to decide who your email is going to be sent to. Picture the people on the list you're planning to use. Think about what their day is like. Think about what is important to them. What are they passionate about? How old are they? What products or services have they purchased from you in the past and why? The more you know about the audience you are writing for, the more targeted and relevant your content will be.

CHOOSE A CATEGORY

It's easier to come up with email content when you think of all your sources in categories. It's also helpful to group the email content you create into categories so you can organize the information into separate emails or separate sections in the same email. That way, you can use different categories of email content to target different interests within your subscriber base. Here are some email content categories you can use to help you in creating, organizing, and targeting content for your emails.

- **Share your expertise.** You are an expert; at least your customers think of you that way. Share your expertise by writing articles, tips, or by answering customer questions.

- **Use facts and testimonials.** Facts about your products or your industry, quotes from customers, stories about their experiences, and even advice from your customers can be effective.

- **Give guidance and directions.** Guiding your customers through steps in a purchase process or giving directions on how to order or how to use your products and services.

- **Offer discounts and coupons.** Discounts, coupons, contests, and giveaways work for some audiences.

- **Exclusivity and VIP status.** Special privileges, VIP status, or exclusivity works for others.

- **Hold contests and giveaways.** You might give a free product or service away to everyone or to one contest winner.

♦ **Acknowledge your audience.** A thank-you note or holiday greeting helps to deepen your relationships.

Content categories also vary by industry. Here are some examples of how the aforementioned content categories might be used by different industries.

♦ Day-Spa: Provide customers with a weekly tip on ways to relieve stress in their lives.

♦ Financial Consultant: Provide clients with a weekly recap of interesting developments in the financial markets.

♦ Nonprofit: Provide donors with monthly updates on the impact programs are having in the community.

♦ Restaurant: Provide customers with fun cooking tips and tricks they can use at home.

♦ Retail: Provide customers with information on special sales (inventory closeouts or new product arrivals) and featured VIP events.

CHOOSE A VALUE PROPOSITION

A value proposition is a statement that explains why taking a specific action, such as reading your email or making a purchase, is more important than ignoring the proposed action. Answer these questions to determine what your value proposition is:

1. Why should your customers buy your product or service?

2. What's in it for them?

3. Why is your product or service better than your competition?

CHOOSE A HEADLINE

If you're going to get your subscribers to read your emails, you need to prompt them to read with a great headline. Your headlines need to grab readers with an obvious "What's in it for me?" message. Ask yourself: "What if they only read the headline? Will they know enough about me and what I offer?"

EDIT AND CONSOLIDATE

After you write your first round of copy, read it out loud. Also, have someone else read it to see if she immediately understands the message. Once your message is clear, decide whether you can cut out any unnecessary copy. One of the keys to great content is to keep it short. When it comes to content, I like to say "be brief, be bright, be gone."

As you edit, cut unnecessary words and consolidate ideas. See if you can get your text down to 30 to 50 percent of what you started with. Also, include bullet points and possibly subtitles to make it easy to read. Make your content easy to scan, as most readers scan a page before deciding whether to read all the details.

Calling for Action with Your Email Content

Calls to action are short phrases, links, and headlines that prompt your audience to take a specific action. Using calls to action can greatly improve the responses you get from your readers.

A good picture may be worth a thousand words, but a good call to action may be worth a thousand sales! There are two primary types of calls to action. In the following sections, I highlight the differences between them and tell you how to use them appropriately.

DIRECT CALLS TO ACTION

Direct calls to action become the direct cause of a sale because they ask for an immediate purchase or a decision that benefits your business financially and immediately. The best direct calls to action have a sense of urgency and leave the recipient feeling that if he doesn't 'act quickly, he will lose out on the opportunity. Examples include the following:

- ♦ Links that add products to a shopping cart.
- ♦ Links that start an event registration process.
- ♦ Links to forms that recipients fill out to order products.
- ♦ Statements that prompt recipients to order by phone.
- ♦ Links that send order information via email.
- ♦ Links that ask for a pledge or donation.

♦ Messages asking for email addresses to send order information.

♦ Links that activate a one-click purchase process or standing order.

It's best to use direct calls to action in combination with promotional emails. It's also a good idea to make sure your audience is ready to buy. You can accomplish both by allowing your subscribers to sign up for specific types of promotional emails when they first join your email list. That way, they are expecting you to ask them to buy frequently.

You can also include direct calls to action in promotions and coupons that you include in informative and relational emails when you follow the rules in the previous section regarding combining objectives.

Another great way to make sure your direct calls to action are appreciated is to create a discount club or convenience ordering process for your repeat customers. That way, your most valued customers continue to feel that they are getting an added value for being loyal to your business. One of my favorite examples of this strategy is exemplified by the Jack-Tar American Tavern in Marblehead, Massachusetts.

Jack-Tar American Tavern in Marblehead, Massachusetts, created an Admiral's Club email list to target customers who needed to be reminded to make reservations or place orders for take-out before leaving work. During the summer, Jack-Tar sends out early bird specials to the Admiral's Club email list members asking them to make an immediate order. The specials are tied to the time of day. If you order dinner before 5:15, then the price of certain menu items for the club members is $5.15. If you order before 6:15, the price goes up to $6.15. This results in significant local traffic at early dining hours and provides added attraction for the tourists who cruise by and see the restaurant packed with customers. They too come in. It's a win-win for the restaurant and it's loyal local patrons.

When it comes to direct calls to action, you want to make sure you do not set the expectation that tomorrow's deal will be better than today's. I saw this in spades during the holiday shopping season of 2008. Many of the big box retail firms sent daily emails during the month of December that started off at a 15 percent discount and gradually increased to the end of the month when many were at 70 percent! Once I had received two or three of these, I waited for the bottom before taking action. I just marked my calendar for a few days before Christmas and then went online and made my purchases. At that point, not only did I get 70 percent off, but also free shipping!

To avoid giving away too much with direct calls to action, make sure you aren't asking too frequently. If your sales cycles are long or if your products or services don't lend themselves well to frequent purchases, you can place your direct calls to action on your web pages and use your emails to drive traffic to those web pages using multi-step calls to action.

MULTI-STEP CALLS TO ACTION

When you aren't sure if your audience is ready to buy or if you want to generate action without asking for a sale directly, you should use multi-step calls to action. Multi-step calls to action ask your audience to take one step closer to a purchase without asking for the purchase directly. Examples include the following:

♦ Links that download a document, audio file, or video.

♦ Links that point to additional information.

♦ Links to set up an appointment.

♦ Links to surveys or information request forms.

♦ Links to maps or directions.

♦ Asking your audience to save, print, or forward your email.

♦ Asking your audience to read your email carefully or scroll to a specific section of your email.

Multi-step calls to action should be followed by direct calls to action, but not always immediately. For example, a golf store might use a multi-step call to action to ask its customers to read a story about golf etiquette on the store's web site. To boost immediate sales, the golf store could place a direct call to action next to the story asking the readers to buy a book about golf etiquette. To boost future sales, the golf store could send a follow-up email to everyone who clicked on the link and read the story. The follow-up email could promote the book and use a direct call to action to ask for an immediate order. Either way, the only people who see the direct call to action are likely to be interested in the etiquette book. This technique helps you to target your offers so your customers don't feel like you're always begging them to buy something.

If your primary objective revolves around building your reputation or brand by sharing valuable information, it's most likely that your calls to action will be the multi-step variety. By using these calls to action you will not only learn what information is of greatest interest to your readers (because you can see when they click on the links), you will also be more likely to keep your content concise.

For example, when I write an article for one of our Email Hints & Tips newsletters, I typically include only the first one or two paragraphs from the article. To view the full article of content, the reader must click on a link to a web page where the rest of the content is stored. This enables us to keep the content short and it tells us which of the articles in a given communication are of greatest interest to our readers.

Inserting Action Links in Your Emails

Inserting links provides your readers with actions they can take while they're in front of their computers, and they provide you with instant feedback because every link in an email is trackable when you use an Email Service Provider (ESP). In this section, I show you how to insert a wide variety of links into emails created using an ESP. I use Constant Contact as an example, but these steps can generally be applied to other ESPs as well.

LINKING TO A WEB PAGE OR BLOG PAGE

1. Type out the call to action that you want to turn into a link. For example, you might type "Read This Article Online."

2. Go to the web page you want to point your link to and highlight the address of that page, including the "http://" and everything after that. Don't just link people to your home page, save them the time and link directly to the page you want them to end up on.

3. Highlight the call to action you typed with your mouse and use your ESP's Link Creation tool to paste in the web page address as the link address.

4. Click Insert to save the link.

5. Preview the email to test the link.

LINKING TO CONTENT WITHIN YOUR EMAIL

When you want people to be able to quickly jump to different sections of your email, you should make your call to action into anchor tags. Anchor tags allow you to link to different parts of your email. For example, you might create a "Back to top" link that, when clicked, brings the reader to the top of your email after scrolling to the bottom. You might also want to create a Table of Contents with links to articles or promotions that appear below the scroll line.

To create an anchor and its associated link:

1. Click on the place in your email where you would like to insert an anchor. If you are creating a "Back to top" link, for example, you should insert the anchor in a block at the top of your email.

2. Click your ESP's Anchor Link tool to name the anchor. In Constant Contact, it's in the left pane under "More Insert Options." In the Insert Anchor box that displays, enter the name for the anchor and click Save. This name will not be visible to your customers. For example, you might name it "top." An anchor icon will display within the block where you inserted the anchor.

3. Click on the place in your email where you would like to insert the link. For example, if you are creating a "Back to top" link, you might want to insert the link at the bottom of your email.

4. Type out the call to action that you want to turn into a link. For example, you might type "Back to top."

5. Highlight the call to action you typed with your mouse and use your ESP's Link Creation tool to tell the ESP that you would like the link to be an anchor link instead of a web link.

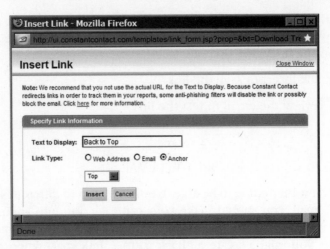

Figure 8.1   Your ESP can help insert anchor links.

6. In the link creation tool, select the anchor you want to link to. For example, "top."

7. Click Insert and save the link.

LINKING TO AN EMAIL ADDRESS

When you want people to be able to send you an email without typing the email address into their email program, you can use an email link to automatically open up the email program on your recipient's computer and insert the email address into the "To" field.

1. Click on the place in your email where you would like to insert an email link and type the call to action. For example, you might type "Email Us."

2. Highlight the call to action text with your mouse, and use your ESP's Link Creation tool to tell the ESP that you would like the link to be an email link instead of a web link.

3. In the link creation tool, type the email address. Example: name@domain.com

4. Click Insert and save the link.

5. Preview the email to test the link.

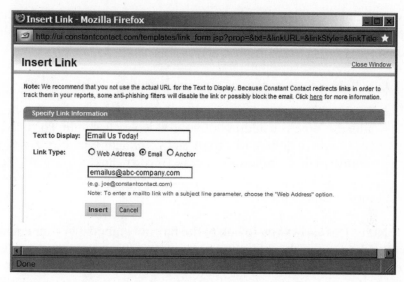

Figure 8.2 Inserting mail-to links is easy with an ESP.

Note: Email links do not track and will not appear in reports, but you'll get an email so you can track them by counting the number of emails you receive.

LINKING TO A PDF OR DOCUMENT FILE

To link to a document, you need to make sure the document is already hosted on your web site. Consult your webmaster if you need help posting files to your web site server.

1. Follow the same steps as creating a web site link.

2. When your ESP's Link Creation tool asks you for the link address, type the address of your document. For example, if your document is a PDF, you might type http://www.yourdomain.com/document.pdf. If the file is a word document, you would type http://www.yourdomain.com/document.doc.

LINKING TO A FLASH FILE, AUDIO, OR VIDEO

To link to a flash file or video, you can point your link to the page where the video is displayed, or you can point your link to the file so the person clicking can download the video to his or her computer.

As with linking to documents, you need to know the address of the file and the file has to be hosted on your web site before your link will work.

1. Follow the same steps as creating a web site link.

2. When your ESP's Link Creation tool asks you for the link address, type the address of your video or flash file. For example, if you're linking to a flash file, you might type http://www.yourdomain.com/flashfile.swf and if you're linking to a WMV file, you might type http://www.yourwebsite.com/movie_location/moviename.wmv

Note: This allows you to link to the file, not embed it in your email. Embedding or attaching files to your email usually causes the email to be delivered to the junk folder instead of reaching your recipient's inbox.

OTHER CALLS TO ACTION

Sometimes the action that you want your recipient to take doesn't involve a link. There are two ways that you can do this and know that the reason your readers landed at your doorstep was your email communication:

1. You can insert a coupon with a special offer made only to members of your preferred email club and ask them to print out the coupon and bring it with them to your store.

2. The greener solution is to insert a code word in your communications that the recipient needs to use at checkout in order to get a special deal. I like to use words that are fun and have nothing to do with the business, like Armadillo. Who said you can't have fun while figuring out who is responding to your communications!

As you can see, there are a lot of things that you can use to engage your audience and have them take action on the content you are sending. No matter what type of communications you are sending, remember to have at least one call to action in every email you send.

9

Looking Professional: Choosing an Effective Email Format

When it comes to creating the right look and feel to your email campaigns, the great news is that Email Service Providers like Constant Contact have already done the heavy lifting for you by designing literally hundreds of different templates to choose from.

Think of each template as a wire frame that you then can customize to your heart's content. You can customize the color, fonts, and even the various blocks contained within the wire frame all without needing any HTML programming skills.

This chapter explains how to choose the right template and construct an effective email layout and design so your content is effectively communicated.

Determining Content-Appropriate Formats

The first step in the process is to select a template that will meet the needs of your communication. There are four basic structures to email templates:

1. **Newsletters** (Figure 9.1). Newsletter templates usually have multiple columns or multiple types of content blocks so you can insert a range of content types and organize them. Newsletter templates also contain table of contents links and some of

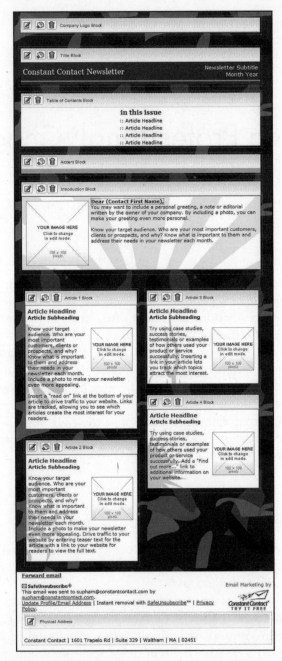

Figure 9.1   Newsletter template

the elements of paper newsletters such as headings and issue numbers.

2. **Promotions** (Figure 9.2). Promotion templates usually have a layout that focuses attention on an image or a headline so readers can identify the promotional message immediately. Promotional templates often have retail or consumer themes.

3. **Announcements** (Figure 9.3). Announcement templates are short and have the ability to quickly relay information under themes such as events, press releases, and business letters.

4. **Cards** (Figure 9.4). Card templates are greetings that can be used for holidays, special occasions, and reminders. They usually look like cards visually and are designed to contain short messages with limited promotional content.

Each template type provides not only a different look and feel but also takes into account the likelihood images and other elements are to be added.

PUT YOURSELF IN THE SEAT OF THE RECIPIENT

It's now time to return to being an email marketing critic of your own email inbox. There are messages that immediately capture your eye and others and create an instant urge to hit the delete button. Depending on the type of communications you are sending, each of the following characteristics might play a lesser or greater role in your final template decision, but they all are important.

Length

The amount of content you plan to include is one of the key elements. While our goal is to keep content as short as possible, there are certain communications (such as newsletters from groups or organizations) where it is desirable to have a number of short articles. In these situations, a newsletter template is typically the best suited. In addition to typically having two columns for content, they also come with a table of contents block that makes it easy for your readers to quickly find content of personal interest.

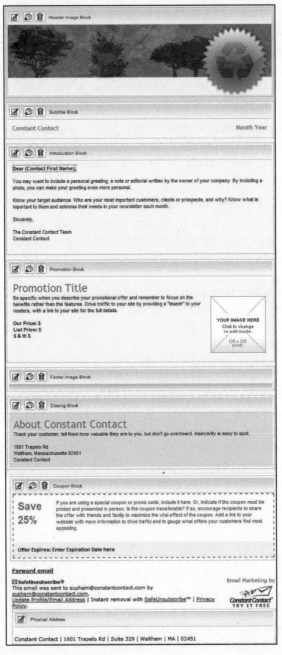

Figure 9.2   Promotion template

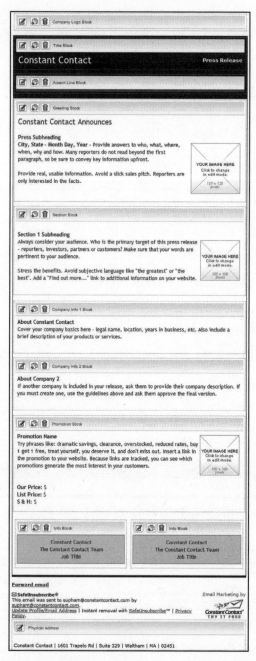

Figure 9.3   Announcement template

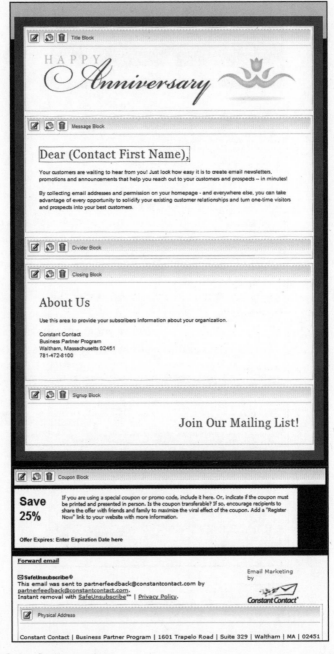

Figure 9.4   Card template

Easy to Read

Factors that make an email communication easy to read include not only layout characteristics but also how colors, fonts, and images are used within the layout.

There are a number of factors working to make an email campaign much more appealing to your readers. The use of color reinforces the content but shouldn't have your recipients reaching for their sunglasses. The font size shouldn't scream at you, and the call to action shouldn't be masked by the colors of the fonts.

Images can help you capture the reader's attention but should not dominate the communication (unless you are an artist or photographer).

White Space

If you are sending a communication with multiple topics or articles, it is important to recognize that you need to give the reader's eyes a break between sections. You can do this by inserting a physical break in the content with a divider, inserting a small image, or just using white space. By inserting several line breaks in your message between sections, each section will stand out, and the reader will have an easier time focusing on your content.

PICK THE TEMPLATE FORMAT THAT DELIVERS YOUR CONTENT IN THE MOST FAVORABLE LIGHT

When selecting an email template, I suggest you try and find a format that will work for the majority of your communications and then spend a little time customizing the look and feel of the communication so that you can re-purpose it every time you send. Remember, part of getting your email opened is having the recipient know who you are. If the look is familiar in preview window, your readers are more likely to open your campaigns.

I mentioned above how newsletters often contain a table of contents. A good guideline is that any communication that includes three or more content sections should include a table of contents. Within Constant Contact, most newsletter campaigns include a table of contents block that can easily be added. This block should be located toward the top of your campaign as shown in Figure 9.5.

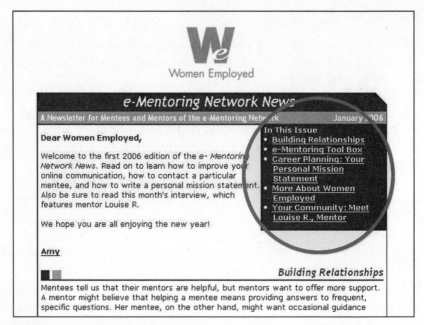

Figure 9.5   Table of contents block

Just Because You Can...

One of our goals in sending great email communications is to keep them short. There is nothing worse than a monthly email newsletter that only comes out once because the writer has used up all of his content ideas in the first fourteen-article newsletter. The same thing goes for promotional campaigns. Just because you can insert images for every product you have in inventory doesn't mean you should. In fact, industry research has shown that over 50 percent of the items purchased from a promotional email are not the items contained within the message.

Email communications are your way of flicking the reader on the forehead and asking them "Hey, do you remember me? And if you do, do you need anything that I have to offer?" If the person remembers you, then odds are she knows what you provide. Therefore, highlighting one or two unique items and leaving the rest up to the reader to explore at your web site or storefront is the best way to get your message across.

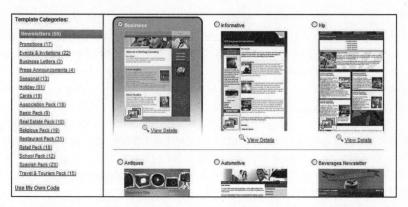

Figure 9.6   Templates can be used for almost any type of content.

You've Got Options

Figure 9.6 demonstrates the sheer volume of preformatted templates available through Constant Contact. Most Email Service Providers also have template pickers to make the process of finding a template easier. However, don't confine yourself to one category of template when searching for your template design. In some circumstances it's a good idea to use promotional templates for short newsletters or event invitation templates for greeting cards. Feel free to explore and find the one that will best meet your needs.

Branding Emails Consistently

Once you have a template layout in mind, you'll need to spend some time adding your colors and logos to the template to make it look like your business. The following sections give you ideas for making your company or organization's communications a consistent brand identity while making them stand out from others.

INSERTING LOGOS AND IMAGES

The logo is one of the design elements that almost all businesses want to include in their communications. In fact, when you set up a Constant Contact account, you can upload your logo once and then it will auto-populate into the logo section in any template that you select. It's that important.

Email templates have placeholders for images also, as shown in Figure 9.7, but you still may want to customize how your logo and images appear in your communications. Because of the need to customize the look and feel of an email, good templates always allow you to put images and logos anywhere in the body of the email even when there isn't a placeholder in the template.

When you insert images into your templates, remember that many of the most popular email programs have preset the account settings so that images are not displayed in the inbox unless the recipient either clicks on a link at the top of each message or changes the settings within his or her account.

What this means to email marketers is that it is important not to include a big image that dominates the top section of your campaign. It's also important not to send an email that only contains an image, because the recipient is likely to see a blank screen, as shown in Figure 9.8.

Since the top of the email is the most important part, and often logos are most useful, I suggest that you use a text bar header that includes your company name and the name of the communication, then include your logo as a smaller design element below that section and off to one side so some text appears before images are enabled by your recipient (see Figure 9.9). That way, your recipient has more confidence in enabling the images to display.

Don't Use Every Color in the Rainbow

Color can be your friend when it comes to email marketing. But there are some downsides to too much color, especially when the colors clash.

When it comes to matching your template colors to your logo, web site, and other branded content, I recommend you use the exact colors from your logo and brand identity. In HTML, your colors have to be "web-safe" and referenced by either an RGB code or a hex-code. If you don't know these color codes, I recommend using a tool like ColorCop (www.colorcop.net) to determine the code for each color you want to use in your email. ColorCop allows you to easily extract an exact color match from any existing online content. Simply take the eyedropper and place it over the color, and it will give you the codes for the colors that you can then use to customize your campaign.

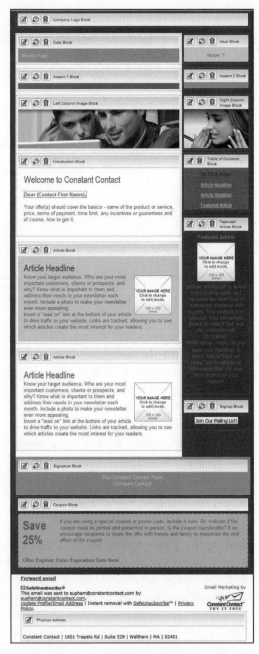

Figure 9.7   Email templates have image placeholders.

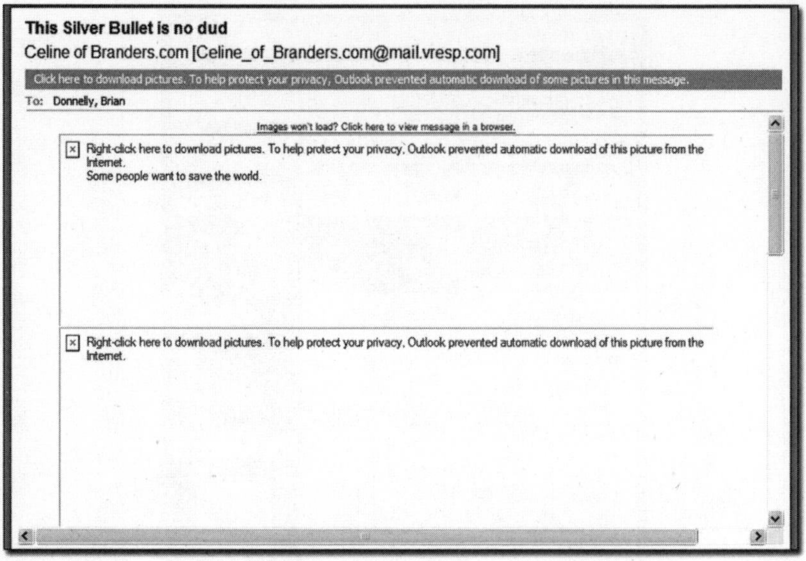

This Silver Bullet is no dud
Celine of Branders.com [Celine_of_Branders.com@mail.vresp.com]

Click here to download pictures. To help protect your privacy, Outlook prevented automatic download of some pictures in this message.

To: Donnelly, Brian

Images won't load? Click here to view message in a browser.

☒ Right-click here to download pictures. To help protect your privacy, Outlook prevented automatic download of this picture from the Internet.
Some people want to save the world.

☒ Right-click here to download pictures. To help protect your privacy, Outlook prevented automatic download of this picture from the Internet.

Figure 9.8   Image size is important due to image blocking.

Using ColorCop is one of the many ways that you can transform one of Constant Contact's templates into your campaign template.

There is another great online tool called ColorSchemer™ (http://www.colorschemer.com) that I like to use to create color palettes for my campaigns. This program allows you to start with your primary color, then provides a variety of colors that you can use to accent the primary color and also for font color selection. Once you have created your campaign, share your design with some honest friends with some sense for colors and ask for their candid opinions.

If you find yourself challenged by designing a look and feel for your email, consider getting help from a professional. Since you are going to be using your email design to represent your business or organization to your clients for a while, it's worth paying a few extra dollars to work with a professional designer. Many marketing agencies and web design firms now offer email campaign creation. You can also enlist the services of your Email Service Provider's professional services team. If you are having a difficult time tracking one down, contact Constant Contact's communications consultants at (866) 876-8464. They can

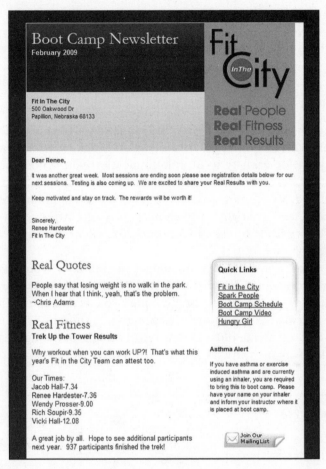

Figure 9.9   Use text along with logos to reinforce your identity.

help you connect with our professional services team or one of our business partners that offer those services.

REMEMBER TO THINK ABOVE THE SCROLL

In designing your campaign, give special attention to the section of the email that's above the bottom of the screen or "above the scroll." The more inviting this section looks, the more likely your recipients will give it the attention you desire. The elements you should be concerned with are large images (logo or otherwise) that may not render with images turned off, the design elements (color, layout, fonts), as well as the content contained in the header and first paragraph. If you are sending a multi-topic newsletter, having your Table of Contents viewable above the scroll is a plus.

REFRESHING YOUR EMAIL FORMATS

You can save yourself a lot of time and increase the likelihood that your recipients will remember you by finding and sticking with a particular email layout for each type of communication you send. I am often asked how often one should refresh the look and feel to keep it from getting dated. My opinion is that your template is helping you reinforce your brand, and changes to it should be made infrequently and in conjunction with the rest of your branding elements (logo, signage, brochure colors, etc).

If you are considering refreshing your brand, I would talk to a marketing consultant. He or she can help you update your brand without negatively impacting the brand equity you have created. Constant Contact recently went through this process, as shown in Figure 9.10.

You can see by the old and new email designs in the figure that we were able to update the look and feel from wavy lines to sharp corners,

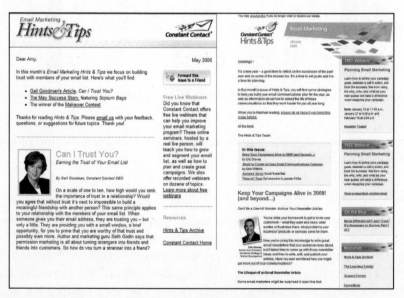

Figure 9.10   Make changes to your brand with care.

and we also made small changes to our logo. We didn't change colors or design elements too much, however, because we wanted to avoid changing anything that hundreds of thousands of people had come to know as our brand.

Ten Email Formats Every Business Should Know About

The next sections provide an overview of the ten most important email formats and how to maximize the potential of each format to generate the desired recipient reaction on your communications.

NEWSLETTER

This format typically has two columns (one narrow, one wide as shown in Figure 9.11). The narrow column is ideal for a table of contents along with either a very brief feature article and logos for newsletter sponsors. It is also a great place to include links to your newsletter archive and a forward to a friend link.

The wider column is where the primary content of your communication should reside. If your newsletter contains more than one topic, you should use section breaks, images, or line breaks to separate the content blocks. Each content block should include a link the reader can follow to learn more about the topic you covered in the content. Links can go to your web site, the web sites of others, to calendars of events, or initiate an email back to you so that you can follow up with additional information.

PROMOTION

This email format is all about making your audience feel special and getting them to your call to action as quickly as possible. Natural instinct is to pile a bunch of images into promotional campaigns highlighting a wide variety of products for sale. However, this is unnecessary. Highlighting one or two special items and providing a strong, time-limited offer will provide you with the best results. You can reinforce your offer message by including a coupon at the bottom of your campaign that highlights the details of the offer as well as how long the offer will be available (see Figure 9.12).

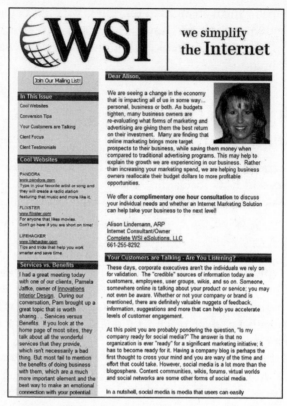

Figure 9.11   Email newsletter example.

EVENT INVITATION

The fact that events are tied to a specific date provides a built-in time sensitivity. Event invitations typically evolve over time with the core message (the event specifics remaining the same) and the call to action evolving. Events typically have three stages:

1. *Save the date:* When the call to action is all about getting your readers to block out time on their calendar.

2. *Registration:* Which sometimes starts with early-bird registration and ends with limited seat availability a couple of days prior to the event.

3. *Post event:* Communications usually follow up with calls to action that include links to materials from the event and a post-event online survey.

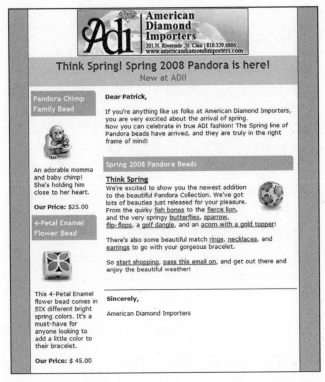

Figure 9.12   Email promotion example

As you can see, there are a lot of communications being sent in a relatively short amount of time. Therefore, it's imperative that you keep your message short and provide a clear call to action (see Figure 9.13).

PRESS RELEASE

A press release can be a great way of spreading interesting news to local media. If this is going to be a part of your communications mix, I suggest you create a separate list for your media contacts and send these communications only to those individuals who have requested this type of information from you. Press releases need to contain content that is worthy of being turned into an article or blurb in a newspaper or magazine. Therefore, do not use this type of communication to try and sell your product. Press releases typically include four sections of content:

Figure 9.13   Email invitation example

1. The headline: A short statement that explains why you are send-ing out the release.

2. The body: Greater detail on the release that covers how and why this news is important, who it impacts, and the details around the timing of the announcement.

3. The statement: Include quote(s) from the impacted parties that reinforce how this information is impacting the community, business, industry, or whatever you are targeting.

4. About you: Typically a boilerplate statement that tells the recipient who you are, what you are all about, and how to contact you.

Writing a good press release is not difficult, but not unlike other email marketing campaigns, you want to make sure that your con-tent is newsworthy in order to keep your contacts interested in reading your content (see Figure 9.14). The press is incredibly busy and they like it when information is buttoned up and delivered succinctly.

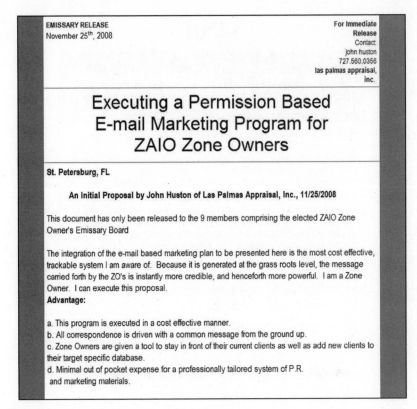

Figure 9.14   Email press release example

ANNOUNCEMENT

Similar in structure to a press release, the announcement is targeted to a different audience. These communications deliver a succinct update on information of interest to your audience. This could be the opening of a new location, release of a new product, or receipt of a distinguished award.

I refer to these as news flashes, and the entire message should be able to be read in the preview pane of your average email client. These communications are typically statements of facts and therefore do not require a call to action (see Figure 9.15).

GREETINGS AND HOLIDAYS

Sending your holiday greeting cards via email is a great way to save money, go green, and still get your message out to your customers

BNI®

BNI Responds to Massachusetts Bar Association Ethics Ruling

Please be advised that there has been an article that was published today at Lawyers Weekly concerning the Massachusetts Bar Association Ethics Ruling. We wanted to let you know that we are aware of the same and are working to get the issue resolved. Adam Bialek, our Attorney from BNI Corporate has already sent an email to the editor of Lawyers Weekly asking for a copy of the "Opinion" which is mentioned in the article.

We also wanted to let you know that we have had similar "Opinion" raised in New Hampshire in 2006, Colorado and Oregon 2008, New York 2006, North Carolina 2005, and that in all situations it has been concluded that it is permissible for attorneys to participate in Referral Organizations after reviewing the findings of the Opinion of the Bar Association for each State.

In the meantime, if you have any questions, please feel free to contact Adam Bialek at 914-323-7000 /Adam.Bialek@wilsonelser.com

To read the Article in question Click Here!

We want to thank you in advance for your patience on this matter.

Figure 9.15   Email announcement example

during the holiday season. In fact, changing over from print holiday cards to email holiday cards can pay for your entire year of email marketing. For example, if you have a holiday card list of 400 contacts, you would likely spend at least $1.50 for each card and postage (not to mention the personalization of each message along with the licking, stamping, and sealing of each envelope). That's a total of $600 for this one communication. By comparison, the cost for an entire year of Constant Contact is $180. Switching to email holiday cards you would save $420 on this one mailing and be able to maintain contact with your customers for the rest of the year for free!

The holiday templates come with a variety of background images, but you can easily swap out any image to include a picture of your employees, new store location, or your logo. Figure 9.16 is an example of one of the holiday templates used for a promotion. You can also use them for greeting cards without promoting something.

Figure 9.16   Email holiday card example

WELCOME EMAIL

Your welcome letter is the first impression you make on a customer. How you handle it sets the stage for your relationship and how well your future email communications will be received. I like to draw an analogy to dating when it comes to your welcome letter. The sign-up form on your web site is like someone asking you to go on a blind date. You don't really know what you are getting into, but you invest a little skin in the game by saying "yes." Your welcome letter is the impression you get when your blind date walks in the door of the restaurant and you lay eyes on him or her for the very first time. It's your first chance to make a lasting impression. so here's how.

When people sign up for your mailing list from your web site, they're showing their willingness to invest in a relationship with you. But you haven't had the opportunity to look them in the eyes, tell them what you're all about, and convince them to do business with you.

Your response to their sharing their email address should be a customized welcome letter that thanks subscribers for joining your community, states your privacy policy, and tells readers how to unsubscribe and change their personal information. You might even want to customize your welcome letter with your logo, web site colors and fonts, and messaging that distinguishes your brand.

Customizing your welcome letter introduces subscribers to your content before your newsletters and promotions are delivered to their inboxes. It creates an expectation for what they can look forward to receiving from you. It also lets you share your enthusiasm for your business and your gratitude to have them join your community. Your welcome letter can include the following:

- ♦ How frequently you send out your newsletter (e.g., the first of every month).

- ♦ What types of communications subscribers can expect to receive (e.g., "our newsletter is full of useful tips and information, announcements about products and services, VIP coupons for valuable savings").

- ♦ A link to your newsletter archive.

- ♦ A "thank you for signing up" coupon to use for their first purchase.

Don't leave your new subscribers hanging. Show them what it means to be in a relationship with your business from the very first connection (see Figure 9.17).

THANK YOU EMAIL

I suggest that on an annual or semiannual basis you send a thank you email to customers with either some interesting new informa-

Figure 9.17   Email welcome letter example

tion on your business or a special gift certificate for being a great customer.

PROCEDURAL EMAIL

Email communications that require a certain action be taken often use very basic email templates. You want the recipient to give her undivided attention to the action she needs to take, and you don't want anything to distract her from completing the task. These communications should contain only one prominent call to action and should be very brief.

An example of how this might be used is when an organization needs all of its members to certify that they have read and agreed to new terms of membership. Once they have read the terms, you simply ask them to click on a link to verify they have read the terms and agree to them. You will then be able to tell which of your members have completed the task and which have not.

SUBSCRIPTION NOTIFICATION/REMINDER

Like the procedural email, subscription notifications and reminder emails typically use basic templates. However, they tend to differ in the call to action since they often don't require action by the recipient but rather simply act to remind them that an event has occurred.

10

Making Introductions: Subject Lines, From Lines, and Frequency

Imagine that you've just heard the phone ring, so you pick up the handset, and suddenly someone on the other end of the line screams, "WE'RE HAVING A BIG SALE!!! WANT TO KNOW MORE?" Then imagine after you say no and hang up the phone that the same person keeps calling every week and shouts the same thing. Wouldn't that be annoying?

Now imagine the same phone call, but this time the person on the line says, "Hi. It's me, Eric, the owner of your favorite golf store. We're having a big sale. Would you like to save 50 percent on a new driver?" Then imagine after you say no that the person asks you if you would like another call when there is another sale.

Whether your emails are more like the unfamiliar and annoying phone call in the first example or the familiar and welcoming phone call in the second example depends on how you write your From line and your Subject line and how often you send certain types of email messages.

This chapter explains how to use your emails to introduce yourself, prompt your audience to open your emails, and determine a sending frequency and length that leaves positive impressions.

Email From Lines: Do I Know You?

It's the first question people ask themselves when an email arrives in their inbox. The answer is a binary yes or no. The From line is all about getting recipients past that first critical step to email success: getting to "yes." Getting to "yes" is essential for email marketing, since "no" is usually demonstrated by an instant delete.

Your From line has two parts:

Part one is the "From Name," such as "Eric Groves."

Part two is the "From Address"—the email address, including the "@" such as, "eric-groves@constantcontact.com."

Your recipients may see just the From Name, just the From Address, or both depending on their email client or reader as shown in Figure 10.1.

In order to get your recipients to recognize you, your email From line has to be familiar. How can you make sure your From line is familiar? The following six tips should help.

1. **Be consistent.** Recipients become familiar with your communications and look for your specific From Name and/or Address in their email inboxes. Consistency in your From Name and

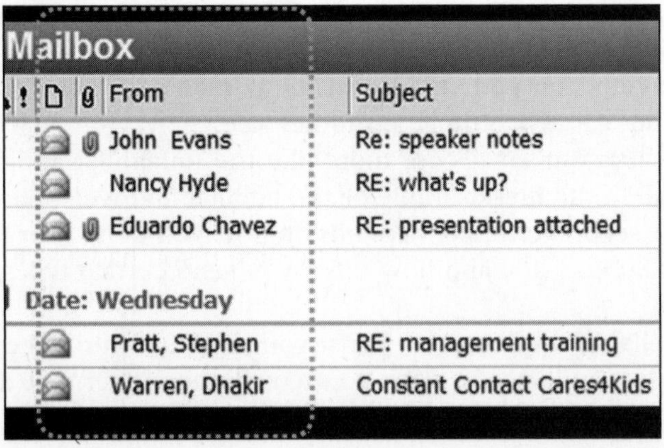

!	☐	🖉	From	Subject
	📩	🔘	John Evans	Re: speaker notes
	📩		Nancy Hyde	RE: what's up?
	📩	🔘	Eduardo Chavez	RE: presentation attached
Date: Wednesday				
	📩		Pratt, Stephen	RE: management training
	📩		Warren, Dhakir	Constant Contact Cares4Kids

Mailbox

Figure 10.1   The From line is visible to email readers and needs to be familiar.

Address will ensure that your email is recognized and opened. Once you have trained your readers to recognize a specific email address as being from your business or organization, resist all urges to change it over time. Recipients typically view their email boxes as being over capacity. Therefore, when they look through their mailbox they are looking to make split second decisions on what to delete and what to keep. This is most often done by sensing whether or not they have a connection with the name associated with the sender of an email. If you change the sender name, you are then asking your recipients to recognize an entirely new entity in a fraction of a second. You run the risk of the instant delete or, worse, being labeled as spam by the recipient. If the recipient flags you as spam in her email, your email will automatically go into the junk folder, never to be seen or heard from again.

2. **Become a trusted sender.** Encourage your recipients to put your From Address in their address book, trusted sender list, or approved sender list (whatever the name may be in their email program).

3. **Make it meaningful.** Both your From Name and your From Address should identify you and/or your company as the sender of the email and clarify the relationship between you and the recipient. Take this opportunity to give the recipient a reason to open your email rather than a reason to delete it.

4. **Use a From Name and Address the recipient will recognize.** Recipients signed up to be on your list. They know your name, your product or service name, or your company name, and are expecting to hear from you. The email address that you choose to send from should contain either the business name or the name of someone that is highly recognizable and associated with the business. It would be nice if you had a lot of room to get across who you are, but you don't. You have roughly twenty characters to get the recipient to remember you. Avoid using generic names that can be associated with anyone such as info@ or sales@. You are just wasting valuable space with characters that say nothing about the sender. In addition, these types of names are often seen as impersonal and therefore containing junk emails. This is another great opportunity to be an email

critic. Take a look at the emails that you receive. Before you click delete, ask yourself what is it about the sender that has you reaching for the delete button. Here are some examples of From lines that range from highly recognizable to not at all recognizable:

- constantcontact@constantcontact.com

- john@johnfinancialservices.com

- chef@restaurantname.com

- info@storename.com

- sales1232@aol.com

5. **Use your brand.** The From line is an important branding opportunity. As such, it is a good idea to use a From Name and/or Address that includes your name, company, product, or service name—whichever the recipient will know best. Your brand in the From line assures the recipient that the email is coming from a reliable and trusted source and builds familiarity and your credibility, especially when repeated over time.

6. Keep your From line short so that it appears in its entirety in the recipient's inbox. If the recipient's email client displays both the From Name and From Address, things can get awfully cramped, and even hidden.

As you examine your From line and consider these tips, remember that there are pros and cons to change. You may already have a From line that works just great for you. You may have a sizable list of recipients who have already added your From Address to their trusted sender list, contact list, or address book. In that case, ""If it ain't broke, don't fix it." However, if you are just starting out or see room for improvement in your From line, now may be the perfect time to make a change.

Subject Lines: Do I Care?

Once you're fairly certain your recipients are going to recognize who you are, you have to give them a good reason to care enough about what you are sending to open and read your email. The first step to getting them to care is writing a great Subject line.

Great Subject lines capture the attention of your recipients and encourage them to open and read your email. They are engaging, informative, and set the stage for the benefit the recipient will gain by taking the time to read your content . . . all in fifty characters.

Writing a great Subject line is no small challenge. You only have a few words to make it compelling, urgent, and specific, without sounding overly "salesy" or misleading your readers. Here are some tips that will help you think about the types of Subject lines that get great results.

1. **Keep it short and sweet.** Do your best to keep your Subject lines under fifty characters, including spaces, as most email clients display fifty characters or less. A recent study done by email monitoring company Return Path showed that Subject lines with forty-nine or fewer characters had open rates 12.5 percent higher than for those with fifty or more and that click-through rates for Subject lines with forty-nine or fewer characters were 75 percent higher than for those with fifty or more. Want to have better open and click-through rates? Keep it short and sweet!

2. **Be specific.** A vague Subject line is a waste of real estate. A great example of this that I see often is monthly newsletters with Subject lines such as "June Newsletter." This tells the receiver nothing about what he will find when he opens the email and gives them very little reason to do so. A better approach for a newsletter like this is, "June Gardening: Three Tips."

3. **Write it last.** Many email marketing services (including Constant Contact) prompt you to write your Subject line first, as you are building your email. I encourage you to come back to it when you are done with your email content. It's important to determine all the elements of your email first and then look for the most compelling topic to highlight in the Subject line. When you are done with the body of your email, read it over and pick the "nugget" that will entice your readers to learn more by opening.

4. **Take some time.** Don't just dash off your Subject lines. Considering how important they are, take some time to think about them and write several before choosing which one to use. Once you have a few Subject lines you like, run them by a friend or colleague and see which she thinks is most compelling.

5. **Test it!** When you have two strong, yet different, Subject lines, test them. Split your list in half and use a different Subject line for each group. After a number of tests like this, you will have a very good idea of what works for those on your list. And as always, the better you know your audience, the more effectively you can communicate with them.

To write a great Subject line, start with what is unique about the content contained within your message. What is the reader going to get out of reading your content? Craft your Subject line around that point. Here are several examples of subject lines that tell you what you are going to get:

♦ Three tips that will straighten your slice

♦ Food donations needed for local families

♦ This weekend's openings—25% off

♦ How to dress for an interview

Each of these Subject lines provides the recipient with the ability to immediately determine what the benefit is for them if he opens the communication. In contrast, here are a few examples from my mailbox of Subject lines that miss the mark:

♦ Hello, Dear Friend!

♦ ARE YOU THE RIGHT PERSON FOR THIS?

♦ Be aware of this

♦ ABJ February 7

♦ Monthly Newsletter

You can also make your Subject lines more engaging by injecting a little humor into them. For example, a catchy subject line for a Certified Public Accountant's newsletter could be "Two tips to get an IRS audit." If you are having fun and being creative with your content, it is likely that your readers will enjoy it too.

Signals like "Three tips" in the Subject line also provide your recipients with an indication that the content is short and to the point. This can be a useful trick to grab the attention of your readers.

Here is a great tip that I use in my inbox. Create two mail folders in your inbox and label them "Subject lines—good" and "Subject lines—bad." Then go through your inbox, deleted, and spam folders and try to identify Subject lines that stand out as exceptions at either end of the spectrum. Put your top picks for both categories in your folders and continue to feed these folders over time. This will become a great resource for you as it fills up with the good, the bad, and the ugly.

Now that you have some of the best practices for writing great Subject lines in mind, here are some approaches you can take to make them even more powerful and compelling.

- **Ask a question.** One of the best ways to get a reader's attention is to ask a question. It's like a trial lawyer questioning a witness on the stand—make sure you get the response you are looking for. "What's the best way to grow your business?" is a great Subject line for business owners. After all, what business owner wouldn't want to grow his or her business? Or let's say you run a health club. An email with the subject line, "How can you lose 5 pounds in one month?" would certainly be compelling. It's important that your question be relevant to your audience.

- **Be a tease.** A clever Subject line can be enticing. When it's done right, readers' curiosity is piqued. They want to know more—and they open your email. Writing a "teaser" style Subject line requires some creativity, and the content needs to deliver on the teaser. A company that sells high-definition televisions could use the Subject line, "You're not going to believe your eyes" as a teaser to introduce a new addition to its product line.

- **Tell it like it is.** Often, what works best is to say exactly what you want your reader to know. Examples of this straightforward approach are, "Sale on all sweaters this weekend," "Master jazz pianist plays live this Friday" and "The seven secrets of a profitable business." This "just the facts" approach works especially well when you can appeal directly to your audience's interests. It also is the best approach to use when you send a newsletter.

- **Remember "WIIFM".** When a person gets your email, the first thing she considers is "what's in it for me?" (WIIFM). She has a decision to make. Does she open your email, leave it for later, or delete it? If there isn't something about the Subject line that lets her know why it's worth her precious time to see what's inside, then the choice will be clear. Delete. Keep WIIFM in mind when creating every aspect of your emails, including the offer, content, images—and most definitely the Subject line. It's all about them. They know that. Just make sure you know it, too!

◆ **Get personal.** The more you can make each contact feel that you are speaking directly to him or her, the more effective your communication will be. Whatever style of Subject line you use, you can make it personal by using the word "you." Professional copywriters know the secret of using this powerful little word. Look around at advertisements, mail, and email you receive, and you will see it's true. Incorporate this copywriting secret when you write your Subject lines and you'll understand why the pros do it—it gets results. A few examples are "Find the right swimsuit for you", "You can save 50% on travel", and "You'd look phenomenal in a custom-tailored suit." (Note: "You" is ideal, but "your" works too!)

Not sure which approach is right for you? Try them all, then show a friend or colleague to get his feedback. Pick the one you believe will be most effective for your audience. Whichever approach you choose, it's always worth spending the time and effort required to write a great Subject line. Because if your readers don't open your email, they'll never have the chance to read the important message you've created for them inside.

You should also spend some time paying attention to your own email junk folder to avoid copying the techniques that spammers use to gain attention for their emails (see Figure 10.2).

Here are the top five ways to look like a spammer:

!	D	@	From	Subject	Received ▽	Size
!	✉		Dan Keyes	Cash credit / Home credit	Sat 9/9/2006 3:1...	1 KB
	✉		acrylate	How to be irresistible to the opposite sex 4179-4	Sat 9/9/2006 3:0...	1 KB
!	✉		Louella	???5?4? ??????? ????????	Fri 9/8/2006 10:2...	3 KB
	✉		Andres Alexan...	Hey you!	Fri 9/8/2006 3:08 ...	697 B
	✉	@	vendor. actual	~~.~Guaranteed Instant Approval!..!	Fri 9/8/2006 3:41 ...	2 KB
	✉		bosonic	Increase sexual satisfactions!!!! 7344	Fri 9/8/2006 1:51 ...	11 KB

Figure 10.2   Avoid spam Subject lines and From lines.

1. Words that come across "spammy" such as free, guaranteed, act now, credit card etc.

2. ALL CAPITAL LETTERS. Looks like you are screaming!

3. Excessive punctuation !!!, ???

4. Excessive use of "click here," $$, and other symbols

5. Misleading Subject lines like "Be aware of this" or "Hello"

Keep in mind that some people save your emails. If you use a descriptive Subject line, you also make it easier for your recipients to find your campaigns in the future. A great email marketing campaign is something that your recipients will want to save. In fact, we suggest in our seminars that nirvana in email marketing is when your recipients create a folder in their inbox just for the emails you send to them. If you can accomplish this and you have great Subject lines, then you will be a resource that they will turn to whenever they need what you provide.

Generic subject lines such as "Monthly Newsletter" make it impossible for the reader to track down a specific article, since the Subject lines all look the same. Be sure to also use descriptive names for your campaigns on your email archive.

Email Frequency and Length: Do I Have Time?

The final question your recipients ask prior to diving into your communications is whether they have time to read what you have to say. Have you ever had a relationship with someone who would just not stop talking? It's exhausting. Relationships need time to develop, and each positive interaction provides an opportunity for the person at the other end of the relationship to respond. Overcommunicating via email can have a negative impact on the trust you build with your customers. So, if you set their expectations to be hearing from you on a monthly basis, stick to it. If you don't, your recipients will eventually lose interest, ignore your communications, and eventually unsubscribe.

The best reputation you can have is for delivering interesting and engaging content that can be read in less than 1 minute. If you are known to ramble on or provide way too much content, then your readers will tend to read your content less often or tell themselves that they will get back to it at a later date. When it comes to email, people rarely come back to something unless the value they receive is significant.

Absence does not make the heart grow fonder when it comes to email marketing. You need to maintain contact with your recipients at least quarterly in order for your relationship to continue to grow. If you fall short of delivering at least quarterly, your recipients will start to forget that they gave you permission to contact them. We like to say that permission is perishable, and you need to stay in touch in order to keep it fresh.

You're communicating to build a relationship, and if you let too much time pass between communications, you also run the risk of your customer forgetting you and turning to someone else. It always amazes me when I hear stories from customers who say that when they send an email campaign the phone rings. At the other end of the phone is typically someone who says, "I am so glad that I got your email, I needed you last week and the email triggered my memory that you do what we need." Your email communications are like reaching out and flicking your customers on the forehead and saying, "Remember me?"

I have worked with some nonprofits to help them understand that communicating once a year when you need to raise funds is not enough. While you may have one or two big fundraising periods, you need to spend the rest of the year sharing the great things that your organization does with the money you raised. The more you communicate the benefits of what you provide, the easier it will be to collect funds the next time around.

When at all possible, set the recipients' expectations for how often and what you will be communicating. I suggest including it in the signup process, in the welcome email, in your campaigns, and on your archive page as follows.

Sign-up Process and Welcome Email

Include on the sign-up form and welcome email a statement that says, "Thank you for your interest in our monthly Staying Fit Newsletter. The newsletter covers one tip per month on ways you can stay fit through stretching along with a special coupon for our VIP customers."

In Your Campaigns

You can provide additional reinforcement of your frequency and primary objective in the body of your email, for example, by simply stating

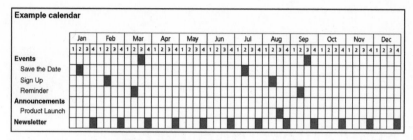

Figure 10.3 Communications calendar

that this month's edition of Staying Fit is about stretches for your lower back. This reinforces your value proposition and the frequency of your communications. It also provides you with the opportunity to solicit ideas for next month's communication.

ON YOUR ARCHIVE PAGE

Including the frequency of mailing and your primary objective on your email archive home page reinforces these points with your existing recipients and also sets the expectations for new prospective recipients that land on your archive.

Once you have set your recipients' expectations for the frequency of your communications, stick with it. If you have set your customers' expectations that you will be sending your communications monthly and then start sending emails on a daily basis, you lose trust in your relationships, and your customers will start to unsubscribe.

A great way to set yourself up for success is to set up a communications calendar (see Figure 10.3). While you don't need to plan out a full year ahead of time, looking at least three months in advance is a great habit to get into. By scheduling your campaigns, you provide yourself with sufficient time to prepare and review your content. In addition, you lessen the risk that you will have a number of communications all going out in the same week. For example, as a wine store you may have a monthly newsletter along with announcements of upcoming wine-tasting events. By creating a calendar you can space out these communications and avoid communications overload.

11

Email Filters and Other Delivery Challenges

Email delivery is a lot like driving. Once you leave the garage, you might find that there isn't much traffic, the weather is nice, and the street is in good condition. Other times an accident reroutes everyone or the road is washed out. Sometimes there's a traffic cop waiting to see if someone is swerving or speeding, and he or she won't hesitate to pull someone over and give him or her a warning or issue a violation.

This chapter covers what happens to your email after you hit send and it leaves the outbox, and it's just like leaving the garage. The email has to overcome many challenges to be delivered to the inbox, including the content of the email, the reputation of the sender, and the characteristics of the technical data included with the email.

This chapter covers the technology behind the delivery of your message as well as some of the ways companies and individuals are using technology to limit the email they receive. It's a fairly technical topic, but it's worth understanding email delivery in every way so you can make sure the majority of your email ends up in your recipients' inboxes.

Email Filtering, Bouncing, and Blocking

When you send an email, it starts out on a server. If you use an Email Service Provider, it sends your email to Internet Service Providers such as AOL or Yahoo! and email programs such as Outlook. These programs and service providers try to sort the email and send only the good email to their customers. When something looks unwanted, they send

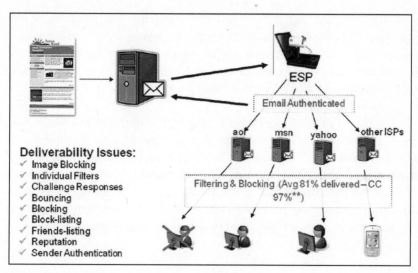

Figure 11.1 Email delivery is a complex process.

it to a junk folder or return to the sender. The process is pictured in Figure 11.1.

Email delivery can be interrupted or rerouted at many points in the delivery process, even when the email reaches an individual's computer. You can't control all the delivery issues you'll encounter, but understanding the challenges inherent in the delivery process is the first step toward maximizing your email delivery. Understanding the process also allows you to recognize errors and correct the ones that are possible to improve.

Understanding the technical definitions of bounced, blocked, or filtered isn't as important as determining the underlying cause of these delivery issues. All of these words mean that the email failed to reach the recipient's inbox. The following sections explain the various underlying issues that cause emails to go undelivered, no matter which technical category they fall into.

(Sometimes you can tell when an email is undelivered and sometimes you can't. You can read more about tracking delivery results in Chapter 12.)

NONEXISTENT ADDRESSES

Nonexistent addresses are addresses that do not exist or have been cancelled. The address may contain a typo, or the individual associated with that address might have left the company. For example, a simple typo like "xxx@constantcontact.con" instead of "xxx@constant contact.com" would prove to be an email address that doesn't exist. In addition to actively cancelled email addresses, many free services cancel addresses that have not been used in as short a time span as three months.

When an email address is nonexistent, the destination email server answers the email with a message that the email address is not recognized as valid. The vast majority of these email addresses will bounce again the next time you send an email campaign, so I recommend that you correct the email addresses with obvious typos and consider deleting the remainder of the addresses from your list or contacting those subscribers with other methods to obtain a valid email address.

UNDELIVERABLE EMAILS

Undeliverable email addresses are email addresses that cannot be delivered because the receiving server is unavailable, overloaded, or could not be found. Therefore, you may find that there are groups of emails with the same domain (the part after "@" in an email address) in this category. Sometimes these problems correct themselves and the emails are successfully sent in subsequent mailings.

MAILBOX FULL

Mailbox full indicates that the email was not accepted because the recipient's email box was over the storage limit. You will not be able to successfully deliver email until the contact frees up some space in the account.

If, over a period of time, the same email address comes up as "mailbox full," it could indicate that the email account has been abandoned or the user isn't checking that email address often.

VACATION AND AUTO REPLIES

Vacation reply or automatic response emails include bounces that were due to an automated vacation message. In this case, the email was delivered. The email recipient has gone on vacation and has set up an automatic "I'm on vacation" email.

BLOCK-LISTS

Block-lists contain lists of domains or IP addresses of known and suspected spammers. If a sender is on the list, its emails likely will be blocked. It is common for an Internet Service Provider to use a block-list to determine which emails should be blocked. Unfortunately, these block-lists also contain many legitimate email service providers and other senders. Just a few spam complaints can land an IP address on a block-list despite the fact that the ratio of complaints to volume of email sent is extremely low.

When Constant Contact appears on a block-list, we contact the ISP or block-list owner and work with that party directly to solve the problem. If you end up on a block-list, you should do the same or use an Email Service Provider who does that for you.

Here are a few popular block-lists and a brief description of each:

SpamCop

This block-list adds IP addresses to its list based on the ratio of spam complaints to volume of email sent. An IP address can be added and removed several times even during a 24-hour period depending on the frequency of sampling by SpamCop.

All email marketing, even fully confirmed opt-in mailings, generate some complaints. So, from time to time and generally for short periods, even Constant Contact is listed on SpamCop. We monitor this carefully and, if a particular customer is causing the complaints, we either help that customer to clean up its lists, or, if it doesn't have a permission-based list, we terminate that account.

SpamHaus

This is a popular and free block-list used by ISPs and corporate networks. SpamHaus also runs ROKSO (Register of Known Spam Operations) that lists spammers who have been thrown off of ISPs three or more times.

FILTERING

Another method for sorting email is called filtering. ISPs filter emails based on their content. Filtered email isn't returned to the sender. Instead, it's moved to a folder other than the inbox. If there are "spammish" terms or phrases used in the "from," "subject," or "body" of the email, a filtering system may sort the email and keep it from being delivered to the inbox. This usually occurs on a per email basis and is typically used by corporate networks and ISPs.

Custom Methods

It is common for ISPs and corporate networks to create their own custom set of criteria for blocking, bouncing, and filtering. Many ISPs use information from block-lists and content filters in a "weighted" system that gives "spam points" for each offensive piece of the message and then sets a threshold appropriate for their system. All email with "spam points" above the set threshold will be tagged as spam, filtered into in the trash, or bounced back to the sender.

Maximizing Delivery: Nontechnical Issues

Making sure your emails are delivered at the highest rate possible is a matter of paying attention to your email content, the relationship between you and your recipient, and the technology you're using to send your email. There are several ways to maximize delivery using nontechnical techniques, discussed in the next sections. I discuss the technical techniques a little later on.

Avoid Spam-Speak

To minimize the possibility that your emails will be filtered out as spam, avoid placing content in your emails that might look like spam to a filter. You'll find spam-like content in the emails in your own junk folder. Check out the spammers to see what they're including in their emails and don't copy their techniques. Here are some of the content elements that are likely to keep your email out of the inbox.

1. Spam Words: free, guarantee, spam, viagra, sex, etc.

2. Spam Phrases: "be amazed," "your income," "subject to credit approval," "earn $$$," "check or money order"

3. Writing in ALL CAPITAL LETTERS (uppercase)

4. Excessive punctuation !!!, ???

5. Excessive use of "click here"

6. $$, **, and other symbols

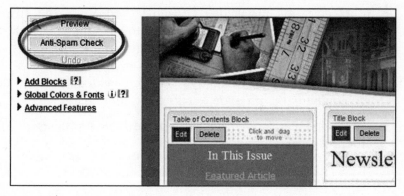

Figure 11.2   Content-scanning tools help you to spot spam-like content.

SCANNING YOUR EMAILS BEFORE SENDING

Some Email Service Providers allow you to pre-scan your emails before sending so you can determine whether the content will look like spam to a filter. Constant Contact developed a content-scanning tool to help increase email delivery rates for our customers (see Figure 11.2).

The tool helps to determine how spam-filtering software might score and process your email. The higher your score, the more likely that your email will not get delivered to everyone on your list. In general, a lower score will increase your email's chance of being delivered to contacts.

Once you scan your email, you can make necessary corrections to your email content, and your email will likely be delivered at a higher rate. However, receiving systems—the ISP or corporate domain, for example—have several ways in which they attempt to block unwanted mail. Content filtering is just one of many ways to prevent incoming spam.

Even if content filtering were the only method being used, it is how the receivers configure spam-filtering thresholds that determines how much email gets delivered, routed to the junk folder, or bounced back to the sender. As a result, even a score of zero in a content scanner cannot guarantee success in the following situations:

1. The recipient's receiving email system chooses to configure its content-filtering software very strictly and prevent most of the incoming email from being delivered directly to customer inboxes.

2. Your recipients installed a consumer version of the spam-filtering software on their computers to scan the email inbox locally. These types of programs usually require their users to initially "teach" the software what to consider "spam." Your emails may not get delivered to these contacts until they train and configure the program to recognize your email.

3. The recipient's receiving email system blocks your email for other reasons.

MAINTAINING ISP RELATIONSHIPS

If you believe your recipient's ISP or email server is blocking your messages despite your efforts to adhere to best practices of permission, content, and reputation, and you are certain that your recipient and the ISP are welcome to receiving your emails, the best way to get your email delivered might be to ask your recipient to contact his or her ISP directly. The following sample letter can help your recipients communicate with their ISPs or systems administrators at their companies.

At Constant Contact, when our customers send letters like these, we can often work directly with the ISPs toward a resolution if more information is required. This not only benefits the sender of the letter, but it can often benefit all our customers if the ISP is convinced that our reputation and dedication to permission are acceptable.

The letters have the ESP contact information removed. If you're a Constant Contact customer, you can find the full text of these letters including the contact information for operations in our FAQ database or by calling our free support line.

Sample Letter You Can Send to Your Recipient

To: Contact
Subject: Contact Your ISP
Hello XXX,

I am emailing to alert you that your ISP is blocking the newsletters/promotions/announcements you have subscribed to receive. I know that you would like to receive these valuable communications, so I ask that you send the attached letter to your ISP's customer support department. Please be sure to replace in the XXXX areas below.

As you may know, Constant Contact powers the email communications I send. When you receive a response from your ISP, please forward the response email to the following address: [ESP email address here]. The Operations Department at Constant Contact will follow up with your ISP once they receive your email.

I apologize for any inconvenience this may cause you.

Sincerely,
XXX

Sample Letter Your Recipient Can Send to the ISP

To: ISP Customer Support
Subject: Remove Constant Contact Block

Hello. My name is XXXX and I have been a customer of your services since XXXX. I understand that you employ filters and/or block-lists to protect customers like myself from unsolicited email. However, this has made it impossible for me to receive newsletters, announcements, and promotions that I have requested. I value these communications and would like to receive them using this email address.

The sender of these emails uses an email marketing service called Constant Contact. Constant Contact is not an open relay and has strict anti-spam policies in place. Because your filters block emails from Constant Contact, I am unable to receive these communications.

I ask that you please help me determine why these emails are being blocked. For further information about Constant Contact or to request more information from them such as log files, the Ops team can be reached at [ESP phone number] or [ESP email address].

Mail from Constant Contact can be found with the following characteristics:

"Envelope from:" domains: [domain names here]

Maximizing Delivery: Technical Issues

There are many technical issues that could cause delivery challenges for your email strategy. These include email authentication and sender reputation. Making changes to your technology can be challenging if you do it yourself. If you send your emails through an Email Service Provider, it may or may not address technical delivery issues. Talk to your ESP to make sure it is doing everything possible to maximize email delivery for you on a technical level.

Understanding the following technical issues allows you to discuss these issues with your service provider or decide whether you have the skills to take on the technical challenges to email delivery yourself. If you're not technically oriented and you find yourself lost in the following sections, skip ahead to the section called "The Benefits of Sending Through an Email Service Provider" so you can determine whether your email service provider takes care of these issues for you.

EMAIL AUTHENTICATION

Email authentication allows an organization to take responsibility for a message in a way that can be validated by the recipient. It is an industry best practice that enables a receiver to validate that a message came from the sender it claims to have come from. This validation means that scams such as phishing and spoofing—which are based on forging the sender of an email—become much easier to detect. Authentication also provides ISPs and other receivers with a validated identity with which to associate reputation data. As a result, authentication can help restore recipients' confidence in the email delivered to their inboxes.

The industry has settled on two basic authentication mechanisms: SPF/Sender ID and Domain Keys Identified Mail (DKIM), which integrates its predecessor DomainKeys with elements of Cisco's Identified Internet Mail. Senders need to implement both mechanisms, since they won't always know which one(s) any given receiver is checking.

Although the basic email authentication technologies have been around for a number of years, it is only recently that there has been significant uptake in the industry. Constant Contact was one of the early adopters: We have had support for SPF, Sender ID, and DomainKeys in our product for quite some time, and added support for DKIM in early 2008.

Microsoft reports that over 90 percent of email marketers are authenticating their email with Sender ID; most major ISPs including Hotmail, MSN, Yahoo, AOL, Comcast, and GMail have implemented authentication on the receiving side. In January 2008 the

Authentication and Online Trust Alliance issued a report claiming that email authentication had reached the "tipping point" and issued a call to action to ISPs and other receivers to start leveraging authentication more strongly in their inbound filtering.

Email authentication has benefits for the following parties:

Email Marketers and Other Senders

It's an industry best practice; it tells ISPs and your contacts that you are a responsible, legitimate sender, taking responsibility for the emails you send. More and more ISPs are using authentication to evaluate the legitimacy of emails. By sending authenticated email, you are solidifying your reputation with ISPs and with your contacts. As you build your reputation over time with ISPs and recipients, their trust in you as a legitimate email sender will grow—and that can gradually improve your email deliverability at the growing number of ISPs and corporate domains that have adopted email authentication.

Receiving ISPs and Corporate Domains

Email authentication helps ISPs and corporate domains determine, with a greater level of confidence, whether an email is genuine or fraudulent and, in combination with accumulated reputation data, whether they should deliver the mail to their customer's inbox.

Email Recipients

Email recipients can have a greater level of confidence in their email inbox. If your ISP or corporate domain uses authentication combined with reputation as a filter, you know that the emails that are authenticated have been properly screened. Recipients are also better protected from various email scams, such as spoofing and phishing.

Everyone

Email authentication can bring trust back to email by laying a framework for legitimate email senders to be reliably identified. With the introduction of email responsibility and identity, we all hope to finally block the spammers who currently hide behind the anonymity of email.

SETTING UP AUTHENTICATION

Setting up authentication is reasonably straightforward for network administrators, but somewhat less straightforward for individuals managing their own domains. The basic requirement is that special records with authentication data need to be published in the Domain Name Service (DNS) entry for the domain that represents your email identity.

If you (as an individual or a company) own and manage your own DNS domain, you can create and publish your own authentication records. Note that having your own domain name does not always imply that you can manage your DNS entry; whether you have that access depends on your domain hosting provider's policies. With this level of self-management, it helps to have an experienced IT department or consultant in order to avoid problems with incorrect or out-of-date DNS authentication entries.

Assuming that you do have access to your DNS entry, you next have to decide which authentication information you want to publish. Sender ID (or SPF) is the simplest way to implement authentication on the sender side, since all it requires is that you publish an accurate SPF record. DKIM is somewhat more complex: In addition to publishing the authentication information, your mail servers (or the mail servers of your ESP) need to be prepared to do the cryptographic signing required by the sender side of the DKIM authentication protocol.

The approach you need to take in order to get this information published will differ according to your specific situation, but most people fall into one of three basic categories:

♦ Using an Email Service Provider (ESP) to send email

♦ Owning and managing your own DNS domain

♦ Using an Internet Service Provider (ISP) account for email

For Sender ID, the record that needs to be published is called the Sender Policy Framework (SPF) record. The SPF record lists all of the email servers that are authorized to send email on behalf of your domain. These servers can be listed explicitly, and they can also be included from an existing SPF record in another domain by including a reference to that external SPF record.

For DKIM, the information that needs to be published in your DNS entry is the public key that receivers will use to validate your DKIM signed messages.

Setting Up Authentication Through an Email Service Provider

If you use an ESP to send your email, you should talk to one of their representatives about what it takes to get your authentication information published. Almost all reputable ESPs already support at least one and often both of the two main authentication technologies and should be able to either publish your authentication records for you or give you guidance on how to publish them yourself if you maintain your own domain name.

We know that many Constant Contact customers may not be interested in managing Sender ID compliance on their own. The Constant Contact Authentication email setting therefore enables you to turn on Microsoft Sender ID as well as DomainKeys, Domain Keys Identified Mail (DKIM), and SPF authentication for your outgoing email with no effort from you other than selecting your authentication domain name.

Sender Reputation

No discussion of authentication in the email industry would be complete without setting it in the larger context of reputation. The huge volumes of spam that plague the Internet make the ability to distinguish legitimate email from spam a critical function for receivers; and, clearly, simply knowing who sent an email (authentication) is not very helpful unless you know something about the sender's identity that allows you to make an assessment of how likely it is to be legitimate (sender's reputation).

One great thing about technology is that it's constantly improving, and spam filters are no exception. In the past, ISPs relied primarily on block-lists (free lists of "bad" senders) and content ("spammy" words) to filter emails. Now they use far more sophisticated technology to collect data that helps them to establish the reputation of the sender. This reputation will, in large part, determine whether email sent from that sender makes it to the inbox, is filtered into the junk mailbox, or dropped all together.

There are two types of sender reputation. The first is that of the Internet Protocol (IP) address (server address) that an email is sent from. The second is that of the domain name (e.g., www.constant contact.com). If you send through Constant Contact, you can rely on the reputation of our IP addresses and in some cases our domain name. Some ISPs look at the "From" address to determine the domain name. In this case they would base your reputation on your domain name (e.g., janet@friendlynanny.com), while others look at the actual domain the email is coming from, in this instance, constantcontact.com.

Yahoo!, Hotmail, AOL, and other ISPs have a variety of factors they consider to determine an IP address's reputation, including:

- **The number of complaints made against the IP address.** This is the number of times that people hit the "spam" or "junk" button. This action identifies emails sent from a certain IP address as unwanted. The ISPs receive such complaints and base that IP address's reputation on them.

- **The consistency in numbers of email sent.** Spammers tend to exhibit erratic sending behavior. They have to keep sending from new IPs addresses to avoid being blocked. In contrast, legitimate senders tend to send from a single IP or small number of static IPs. If an IP address shows "spiky" behavior, it damages its reputation with the ISP.

- **Unknown user rate.** This is the rate of emails in a send that are sent to nonexistent email addresses, also known as bounces. High numbers of bounces to these defunct addresses will have a negative impact on reputation.

- **Spam trap hits.** A spam trap is an email address created by an ISP that is not publicly available. It can only be found by computers that are harvesting email addresses from the Web. These computers are also known as spiders or web crawlers. ISPs recognize IP addresses who send mail to these "trap" addresses as spammers.

At present, the IP reputation is the primary factor considered by the ISPs, but the importance of domain name reputation (the second sender reputation) is on the rise. A significant step in building one's reputation leads back to authentication. When a domain name is authenticated (or validated) by an ISP, it provides the ISP with a reliable identity on which to build the sender's reputation. Think of it like building good credit. Your credit is tied to your social security number. In this case, your reputation is tied to your domain name. With credit, if you play by the rules and exhibit best practices, you can get loan approval and that shiny new car. When you have a good domain reputation, you get ISP approval and the reward of emails delivered to the inbox.

While no ISPs have made authentication an absolute requirement for incoming mail, they are rapidly moving in this direction. That's why it is in your best interest to make sure your email is authenticated.

THE BENEFITS OF SENDING THROUGH AN EMAIL SERVICE PROVIDER

When you send through an ESP's shared IP addresses and domain, you benefit from a reputation and a high delivery rate that is fought for and protected every day. In the case of Constant Contact, we have a team committed to deliverability and another to compliance. These groups work closely together to make sure our IP addresses and our domains have great reputations.

Maintaining a good reputation requires that we set high standards and are selective with who can mail through us. For example, we require our customers to use permission-based email lists. When our team sees signs of a purchased or harvested list, they contact the customer to get more information and sometimes must close an account. This is one of the hardest things we have to do, but keeping our customers' delivery rates high is our number one priority.

12

Tracking and Improving Email Campaigns

One of the greatest challenges of marketing in general is understanding the actual impact generated by a specific marketing effort. Email marketing, when done through an ESP, solves that challenge because within minutes of sending a campaign, you're able to immediately see what happens to your messages. This chapter highlights the information that Constant Contact collects and reports back to you that helps you market smart, time after time.

Why Tracking Is Important for Building Relationships

When you are building a relationship face to face you have the ability to look the other person in the eyes to gauge how she is reacting to what you are saying. Being able to read her reactions provides you with the ability to know if she is engaged in what you are saying, if you should be changing the subject, or if you are making a connection. When it comes to email marketing, you don't have the ability to look your recipient in the eyes, but through tracking you can tell if you are making a connection!

It Takes the Pulse of Your Readership

When you send an email marketing campaign through a service like Constant Contact, you get a wide variety of feedback on whether your campaign made it to the recipients, if they opened the campaign, and whether they clicked on one or more of the links contained within the message. This information provides you with the relationship pulse of your recipients. By reading this chapter, you will learn how to interpret whether the strength of your relationships are growing, declining, or remaining unchanged. You will also know whether you are building trust.

It's important to note that your readers may not be aware of all of the great insight you have with regard to the relationship because of the feedback you receive. While this information helps you understand the state of your relationships, it's important to not freak out your recipients by telling them all that you know. For example, calling a recipient and asking him why he just clicked on a link in your last campaign might not result in the building of trust.

IT HELPS YOU DETERMINE THE CONTENT THAT RESONATES BEST WITH YOUR AUDIENCE

Through tracking you are able to determine the rate at which your communications are being opened and to a certain extent determine what content was of interest to your readers and what content fell flat. By knowing this information you can then tailor your future content to focus on the areas of greatest interest while steering clear of those topics that just did not resonate with your audience.

If your communications contain more than one topic, you will be well served by including only the introductory paragraph of each topic within your email and then including a link to your web site or archive where the full content can be found. This will enable you to see how many people are clicking on the links to read the full content on each topic, providing you with great insight into which topics resonate the best.

When you use this information to eliminate unwanted content, you are not only able to focus on topics of interest, you can also shorten the amount of content you send!

IT HELPS YOU IDENTIFY AND REWARD YOUR BEST CUSTOMERS

The pinnacle of relationship building is the formation of trust. Trust exists when your customers are willing to put their reputation on the line for your business. One of the great tracking elements of email marketing is that you can see when someone forwards your message along to a friend by using the Forward to a Friend link within your campaign. While you can't see who someone sends it to, you can see who forwarded your message and how many people he or she has sent it to. These are people that you need to find a way to thank. There are numerous ways that you can thank this audience. Again, you don't need to let them know that you are monitoring their behavior. However, simply adding them to your VIP email list for inclusion in special offers or invitations to VIP events at your charity or organization can serve as a suitable reward.

How Tracking Works

Email Service Providers can help you track lots of positive and negative results, even if your audience doesn't directly respond, and you can track direct responses back to specific individuals. Here's how it works.

When you send an email, your Email Service Provider automatically adds special code that enables the tracking of certain responses. It's possible to track

♦ Which emails bounced and why they bounced.

♦ Which emails received spam complaints.

♦ Who opted out of receiving future emails.

♦ Who enabled the images to display in their email.

♦ Who clicked the links in your email.

♦ Who forwarded your email to someone else.

ESPs collect and aggregate the tracking data from your emails and generate a tracking report so you can see the tracking information in an easy-to-use format (see Figure 12.1).

Email tracking data can be a bit confusing because tracking requires a combination of technology and human interaction, and both have certain limitations. The following sections show you how tracking works so you can understand the limitations and gain a realistic perspective on what your tracking data actually means.

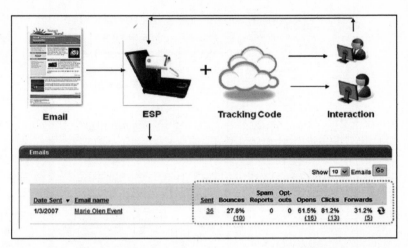

Figure 12.1   Email tracking reports show you tracking data resulting from your email.

DELIVERY TRACKING

Your Email Service Provider can't tell you whether a specific email was delivered to a specific recipient's inbox, or any email folder, for that matter, without some sort of interaction from the person receiving the email. Some ESPs publish a delivery rate, but be careful about how they calculate that number. Some ESPs tell you they have a 97 percent delivery rate, for example, but they really mean that 3 percent of their emails bounce back on average, so they just assume 97 percent are delivered.

True delivery to the email inbox can be measured by a third-party service called Return Path. If you use an ESP who measures delivery through this service, you can trust that your email delivery rates will be about the same as the ESP's delivery rate. If your delivery rate is higher or lower than the ESP's average, it probably means the quality of your email list or email content is above or below average.

BOUNCE AND BLOCK TRACKING

It can be difficult to tell why an email bounced if you're not a computer, because the program that returns the bounced email to your inbox usually attaches computer code to the bounce message to tell you why the email was undeliverable (see Figure 12.2).

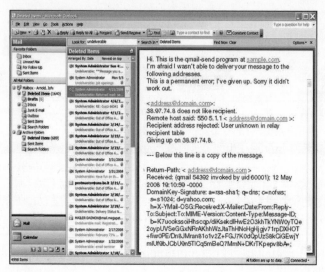

Figure 12.2   Bounced email code is difficult to read if you're not a computer.

When you use an ESP to send your email, bounced email is returned to the ESP's computer so the ESP is able to generate a report that a human can read. The report tells you why your emails bounced and displays them in categories so you can take action on the information in batches (see Figure 12.3).

The bounced email report let's you see which emails bounced, why they bounced, and which emails were blocked. Some emails

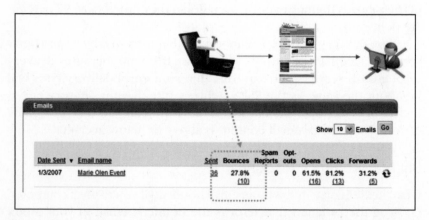

Figure 12.3   Bounce reports help you identify delivery problems for specific emails.

are returned to the sender with no code or nonstandard code. These bounced emails are usually placed in a category such as "other."

OPEN TRACKING

Emails that are "opened" are tracked by hosting images on a server and embedding the hosted images in the body of the email. When the image displays in the email, the server hosting the image has to "serve up" the image, and the server gets a hit. So, the email isn't really "'open"—it just means that the images in the email are displayed.

If you don't have any images in your email, your ESP puts a blank image in the email in order for open tracking to work. The image can't be seen by the recipient, but it can still be enabled when recipients enable images to display in their inboxes.

Open rates have been trending down over the years, but not because fewer people are reading emails. It's because fewer and fewer email programs are displaying the images in emails automatically. This means individual recipients are getting used to scanning and reading emails without enabling the images to display.

CLICK TRACKING

When someone clicks on a link in your email, you can track the link by adding tracking code to the link. ESPs insert tracking code automatically so you don't have to code every link and write a program to capture and report on the information.

Many marketers use their click-through rate as a judge of whether the email was successful, because it indicates that people were interested in the email, and the email was able to drive traffic toward the place where the link points.

FORWARD TRACKING

When someone uses her email program's forward button to forward your email, you can't track it reliably. You can track forwards, however, by inserting a special forward link in the body of the email (see Figure 12.4). Forward tracking links work the same way as regular email links.

Forward tracking is a good way to determine whether your email content is valuable because people won't forward your email to a friend or colleague unless the content is valuable enough.

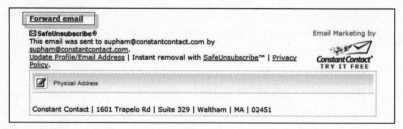

Figure 12.4   Inserting a forward button in your email enables forward tracking.

UNSUBSCRIBE TRACKING

When someone wants to be removed from your email list, you are required to take him or her off your list permanently. The best practice is to provide an unsubscribe link so people can remove themselves automatically. One benefit of providing a link is that you can automatically track the number of unsubscribes and use the results to determine whether you need to adjust your strategy.

SPAM REPORT TRACKING

Some email programs contain a "spam" or "junk" button that people can use to identify emails as spam or junk. When someone uses one of these buttons, it reports the email as spam to the email program's systems administrator. For example, Yahoo!, AOL, and Hotmail all provide these buttons to their customers.

Since the spam or junk buttons report complaints to the company that supplies the email program and not to the sender of the email, many ESPs have formed relationships with the companies who provide these buttons to their customers so they can report spam complaints back to their customers. These relationships are known as "feedback loops," and they typically operate with a certain degree of anonymity. That means if your ESP has feedback loops, you probably won't know who complained about your email, but you will know how many people complained.

What to Do About Tracking Data

Once you understand how tracking works, you can analyze the data and improve your strategy. As with any data analysis, you need to make sure you are paying attention without overanalyzing so you spend more time improving your strategy and less time steeped in numbers.

The following sections tell you how to analyze and take action on the tracking data supplied by your ESP by applying Constant Contact's perspective to the information available to you through tracking reports.

HANDLING INDIVIDUAL BOUNCED AND BLOCKED EMAILS

In Chapter 11, I discussed the measures you can take on an aggregate level to improve your email delivery in general, but you also need to take action on the bounce and block data related to specific emails.

Tracking bounced and blocked emails after sending is important so you can determine which customers or prospects were unable to receive your message for certain technical reasons.

When an email address is nonexistent, or no longer valid:

♦ It's called a "hard bounce." The email is either misspelled or the user has changed his or her address.

When an email is undeliverable because the server was down, the mailbox was full, or the email blocked:

♦ It's called a "soft bounce" because these events could be temporary.

When your bounce report tells you that an email address is nonexistent, or no longer valid:

♦ You can check for obvious misspellings. For example, an email address that ends in "@hotmail.comm." can be easily corrected. If it isn't obvious, don't guess. Email addresses can be odd, and you don't want to mistakenly send someone an email he or she didn't ask for.

♦ You can contact the subscriber for new or corrected information or delete him or her from your list if you aren't able to determine whether the email is misspelled. It's a good idea to collect alternative contact information from your customers in case they change email addresses without notifying you.

When your bounce report tells you that the server was down, the mailbox was full, or the email was blocked:

♦ You can try to send the email later and watch for trends.

♦ If the emails get through after trying again or making alterations (i.e., sending a text-only version of your email), make note of the changes or start a separate list for email addresses with known issues.

♦ If the emails repeatedly bounce, you'll probably have to obtain a new address if practical.

IDENTIFYING TRENDS IN OPENED EMAILS

An email tracking report shows you the number of emails that were opened and who opened them. Since an email is only considered "open" when the recipient can see the images in the email, you shouldn't judge the success of any one email based on the open rate alone. Instead, watch for trends in your open rates over time.

If Your Open Rates Are Trending Down:

♦ Fewer subscribers are enabling images
   ○ Use text that invites your audience to enable images—tell them it's safe or make the images sound important.

   ○ It could be an indication of subscriber boredom or delivery problems—watch for clues in emails with higher or lower open rates. Was there a particular link, Subject line, or image that increased interaction?

If Your Open Rates Are Steady:

♦ Assume the email is being received
   ○ Unless you have hard data to indicate otherwise, such as a bounce report showing that the email was undeliverable.

♦ Check your ESP's average delivery rate
   ○ If you're using an Email Service Provider, ask for its delivery rate and make sure it's been verified by a third party. Average delivery rates tend to be around 80 percent, but some Email

Service Providers deliver email at much higher rates. (Constant Contact's delivery rate is consistently above 97 percent.)

If you have viewed your open rates, and they don't compare to your industry's average open rates, you might want to take the following measures to try and improve it.

♦ Use a recognizable From Name. Make sure you use a From Name and Address that includes your name, company, product, or service name—whichever the recipient will know best. When you repeatedly brand the From line like this over time, you ensure the recipient that the email is coming from a reliable and trusted source and builds familiarity and credibility.

♦ Grab recipients with the Subject line. Make sure the subject is short and to the point, between thirty and forty characters and no more than five to eight words, and state a clear benefit to opening the email. Make sure the Subject line does not look like spam. You do not want to use any unnecessary punctuation, all capitals, or have your email come across as a trick or gimmick.

♦ Target your audience. Send a short survey to learn more about your audience. You can then segment your audience by saving respondents with similar interests and preferences into new contact lists.

♦ Consider your delivery day and time. Industry statistics suggest that recipients are more receptive to offers in the midday, midweek timeframe.

♦ Evaluate your email list. Over time, the people on your email list may become less interested in your emails for one reason or another.

EVALUATING CLICK-THROUGHS

The links in your email give your audience an opportunity to interact with your message. Links can be pointed to

♦ Any page on your web site, blog, or social media page.

♦ Any file hosted on your web site server such as a PDF document or an audio or video file.

♦ An online survey or a poll.

♦ An email address so you can direct your audience to a specific email addresses instead of replying to the email address where the email came from.

When you look at a tracking report, you'll be able to see the number of clicks in each email campaign (see Figure 12.5).

You can also click to see more detailed information, including which links were clicked and who clicked them. Use your tracking report to determine the following:

Audience Interests

♦ Clicks tell you what topics were interesting. For example, a golf retailer that sells special golf clubs for kids under 12 can assume that anyone clicking on a link to learn more about the clubs has kids under 12.

♦ Save clickers in an interest list for targeted follow-up. When you know who is clicking on your links, you can save them as a

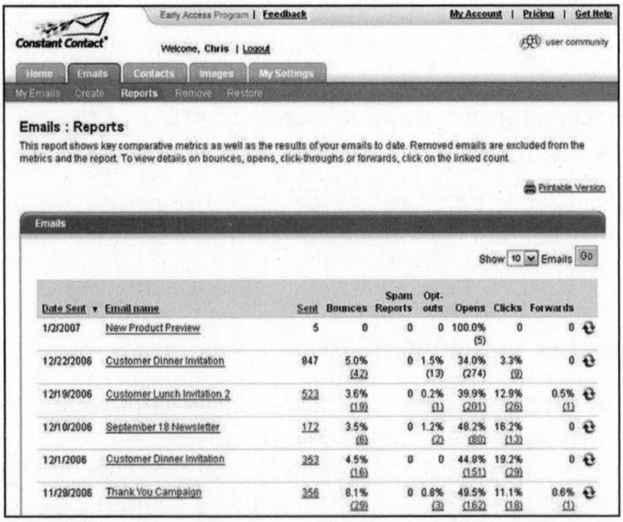

Figure 12.5   Tracking reports show you the number of clicks for each email and individual links and clickers.

separate list for more targeted follow-up. In the golf example, the retailer could begin to include kids' promotions and golf tips for kids in future emails to the interest list.

Goal Achievement

♦ Use links to drive traffic toward conversion. Make sure every link moves the clicker closer to making an immediate purchase (or other decision) instead of distracting him or her from the ultimate goal.

♦ Compare clicks to conversions and improve. If your email resulted in a lot of clicks and a low number of completed purchases or "conversions," your email was effective in driving traffic toward conversion, but your web site, store, or sales process isn't working. If your email doesn't receive very many clicks but you have a high conversion rate, your sales process is effective and your email message needs attention to drive more traffic. (You can track conversions with web site analytics or by comparing the number of emails sent to the number of purchasers who responded to the message in your email.)

You can increase the number of clicks on your email links overall when you have a strong call to action, good copy, and a compelling offer in your email. Make sure your email describes the benefits and rewards for immediate action.

Here are some hints that will help you troubleshoot and improve your click-through results going forward:

♦ Review your call-to-action. It may not be strong enough or clear enough.

♦ Review your copy. It may be too long, keeping your offer from standing out. Stick to simple words, short phrases, and paragraphs of one to three short sentences.

♦ Review the Subject line. Does your offer fulfill the promise of your Subject line?

♦ Review your overall email. Did you set your contacts' expectations appropriately?

♦ Make sure you have created a sense of urgency. Limit the offer to a specific time period or, for example, the first fifty customers. If you're using a time period, quantify it (e.g., "until November 23rd" vs. "for the next two days").

Note: It's important to remember that email marketing is not an exact science; it is an ongoing learning process! Keep reviewing your statistics and making the necessary tweaks to improve your next mailing.

UNSUBSCRIBE REQUESTS

When someone wants to be removed from your email list, the best practice is to remove him or her immediately and permanently. If you use an Email Service Provider, it can automatically handle unsubscribe requests by placing people on a "do-not-mail" list when they click your unsubscribe link.

Consumers unsubscribe when they

♦ Feel that they are receiving too much information. Either too many emails or too much content in each email can increase unsubscribe requests. Include only essential information in your emails and use a spreadsheet or calendar to plan your email campaigns so you leave reasonable time in between emails.

♦ Feel that your content is irrelevant. Watch your click reports and use surveys to keep track of your audience's interests. Remember that your audience isn't always interested in the same things that you are.

♦ Feel that your content isn't intended for them. For example, sending discounts and coupons to your audience when they are really interested in higher quality and willing to pay for it.

To help you keep track of trends and determine the most common reasons for unsubscribe requests, offer your unsubscribing customers and prospects a comments form so they can tell you why they want to opt out of your communications (see Figure 12.6).

You can help reduce the number of unsubscribe requests you receive by monitoring your tracking reports routinely and taking the following actions.

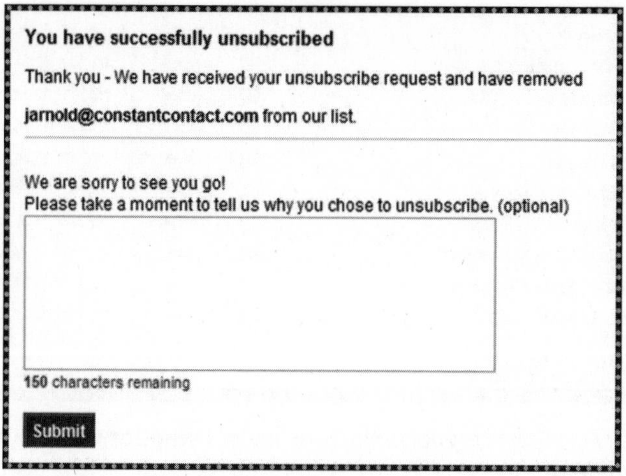

> **You have successfully unsubscribed**
>
> Thank you - We have received your unsubscribe request and have removed
>
> **jarnold@constantcontact.com** from our list.
>
> ---
>
> We are sorry to see you go!
> Please take a moment to tell us why you chose to unsubscribe. (optional)
>
> ```
>
> ```
> 150 characters remaining
>
> [Submit]

Figure 12.6   Offer a comments box when customers unsubscribe.

♦ Use an instantly recognizable From Email Address and From Name, accompanied by a clear and relevant Subject line. Two of the most common reasons for recipient spam complaints are failure to recognize the email's sender and failure of the email content to match the expectations the subscribers had for the subject matter and frequency when they opted in to the list

♦ Back off on your frequency. If you're sending too many emails without leaving adequate time in between them, you could be overcommunicating.

♦ Reduce your content. People generally don't like long emails. Shorter information is less likely to be perceived as bothersome by people who aren't interested in your content the moment they receive your email.

IMPROVING EMAIL FORWARDS

Your audience can forward your emails using the forward button in their email program, but it's better to provide a trackable forward link in your emails so you can identify the people who forward your emails and use the reports to watch for trends (see Figure 12.7).

When someone uses the forward link in your email, you won't see the private information belonging to the person who receives

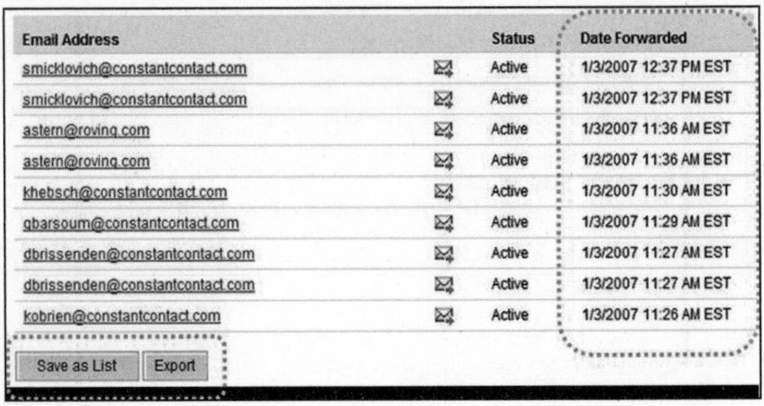

Email Address		Status	Date Forwarded
smicklovich@constantcontact.com	✉	Active	1/3/2007 12:37 PM EST
smicklovich@constantcontact.com	✉	Active	1/3/2007 12:37 PM EST
astern@roving.com	✉	Active	1/3/2007 11:36 AM EST
astern@roving.com	✉	Active	1/3/2007 11:36 AM EST
khebsch@constantcontact.com	✉	Active	1/3/2007 11:30 AM EST
gbarsoum@constantcontact.com	✉	Active	1/3/2007 11:29 AM EST
dbrissenden@constantcontact.com	✉	Active	1/3/2007 11:27 AM EST
dbrissenden@constantcontact.com	✉	Active	1/3/2007 11:27 AM EST
kobrien@constantcontact.com	✉	Active	1/3/2007 11:26 AM EST

Save as List   Export

Figure 12.7   Forward reports show recipients who forwarded the email to someone else.

the forwarded email on your forward report, but you will see who forwarded your email and how many people they forwarded the email to.

At a minimum, make sure you are thanking people for helping you spread the word about your business. You can also use your forward report to:

♦ Learn about the value of your email content. When your forwarding increases, try and figure out what caused the increase. Was it a specific topic, product, or offer that increased the activity?

♦ Thank people who forward your emails. When someone repeatedly forwards your emails, you have a valuable advocate for your business. Make sure you thank him or her.

Sometimes you can increase your forwarding just by asking your audience to help you spread the word. If you don't ask at all, you aren't likely to get many forwards. Here are a few more tips on getting the best results from your forwarded emails.

♦ Use an ESP that formats your forwarded emails correctly. Email programs are notorious for reformatting the HTML in a forwarded email. A forward link sends a completely new copy of the email directly to the forwarded email address so the email isn't reformatted by the recipient's email program.

♦ Enable the people who receive your forwarded email to join your email list. When your subscriber forwards your email using the special forward link, you can make sure the person who receives the forwarded email gets a special message that tells him or her about the value of the email list the email originated from.

13

Collecting More Feedback with Surveys

"Feedback is a gift" is a quote often used around the halls of Constant Contact. When it comes to building and maintaining relationships, there's no better way to know how the relationship is going than to ask. With over 250,000 customers, this might seem like a daunting task; however, it's something our entire company looks at on a monthly basis.

We send a customer satisfaction survey out to one-twelfth of our customers each month. That way, we ask all of our customers for their feedback only once a year, but we get regular monthly feedback on how we are doing. It's a wealth of information, and for a company that's laser-focused on delivering an exceptional customer experience, it's mission critical.

In this chapter I cover the benefits to your business of using your emails to ask survey and poll questions, and I show you how you can obtain regular feedback, set yourself up for feedback success, and use the information you receive to grow your business even more.

The Benefits of Ongoing Feedback

In the movie *What Women Want,* the main character, played by Mel Gibson, learns the distinct benefit of having real-time feedback by reading the minds of the women he's interacting with. While this represents an extreme form of feedback, it's clear that the more you know about what the person on the other end of the relationship is thinking, the greater the likelihood that you are going to be able to deliver what he or she is looking for.

While it's unlikely you have the ability to read the minds of your customers, the next best thing is asking for and receiving feedback from them. In the next sections, I highlight the benefits you and your business can receive by asking for the gift of feedback from your readers.

FEEDBACK GIVES YOU A COMPETITIVE ADVANTAGE

Gathering feedback from your customers during the various stages of relationship development provides you with greater awareness of their needs and puts you in the best position to deliver the right solution at the right time. Gathering regular feedback is a best practice for any email marketing strategy; however, its importance is amplified in situations of uncertainty and change.

Feedback is your ability to keep your finger on the pulse of your customer relationships. If you are collecting it regularly, you will be able to get an early sense for changing trends and then will be able to monitor their development. This insight enables you to reposition, repackage, and redirect your business so that you are more closely aligned with the changing needs of your customers well ahead of the competition.

Feedback at the point of connection is a great way to gain insight into how your best new customers are finding out about your business. Did they come through a referral from an existing customer or find you through a search query on their favorite search engine? This type of feedback can help you channel your efforts to beat your competition to the next new customer.

FEEDBACK HELPS YOU MAKE GOOD DECISIONS

When you know where your best new customers are coming from, you can use that information to tailor your email marketing program so that you are adding new customers at the lowest possible cost of acquisition. This provides you with additional monies to be spent serving your customers, acquiring new customers, or investing back into your business. This information is extremely valuable when you need to make informed decisions on where to either cut back while minimizing the impact on your business or alternatively where to spend more to gain market share.

Businesses and organizations often host events as a way to draw existing customers back to the business and to introduce new potential customers to the value you bring in an interactive environment. In advance of spending the money to put on an event, one of the best ways to maximize the potential outcome is to get some feedback on what type of event would be of greatest interest to the individuals you are trying to attract. For example, a wine store could survey its customers to determine whether they are more interested in a wine tasting of French Bordeaux wines or Californian Cabernet. In addition, it could ask its audience if they would be more likely to attend an event if it were held on Thursday evening or Sunday afternoon. By collecting this feedback, the wine store can avoid the event of least interest in favor of the one that their customers are most interested in and avoid a costly mistake.

It Helps You Deliver Highly Relevant Content

I believe that every email marketing communication should include at least one feedback mechanism through which your readers can respond to you. It's also a great way to get content ideas for your next communications. By encouraging your audience to tell you what they would like you to educate them about, you are sure to deliver something of value to them. You can also create a more structured request for information that highlights five potential topics that you could cover and asks your readers to rate them in order of their interest. You can respond to your readers with the content of greatest interest first and let them know that they asked for it and you delivered. That's a great way to build trust in a relationship!

Another great thing to do with feedback that engages your audience in the content is to credit them for their suggestions. Add a section to your email that challenges your readers to try and stump you, then select an award winner each month with the best question. This not only provides you with great content ideas, it also encourages your readers to open your email to see if they won.

In addition to writing more interesting content, you can also use feedback to segment your list into interest groups. For example, a sports store owner with one general list of contacts could use an online survey to ask its customers about their sports interests. It can then use this information to send special offers regarding Callaway golf equipment to the audience that provided feedback that they were golfers.

The more closely tied a communication is to the interests of the reader, the more likely he or she is to open it, read it, and forward it on to others.

How to Ask the Right Questions

Whether you use surveys, polls, or simply ask your customers to email you their feedback, there are plenty of things that you probably want to know. The key is focusing in on what you need to know. Asking your customers to answer too many questions might drive them away, so cut out the clutter and ask only when the information is critical.

The following sections provide guidance on which questions to ask and how to ask them.

START AT THE END

The best starting point for asking the right questions is the end point. At the end of the day, you are collecting information so that you can make an informed decision and take action. So what is it that you want to make more informed decisions about? By defining the problem you are trying to solve, you will then know what information you need to collect in order to make an informed decision.

You may feel the urge to now jump right into generating your questions, but there is one more step. The final step is to determine what needs to be measured in order to give you the information you need in actionable format. Now that you know what you are going to measure, you are in a great place to start creating questions that will give you great feedback.

Here's an example of how this might play out in a real-life situation. A wine store has seen the attendance at its wine-tasting events decline over the past several months. The owner is perplexed about the reason for the decline and has made the decision to get some feedback from her customers. Here are the steps she goes through in creating an online survey:

Step One: Decision / Action

She wants to know why the attendance has declined and what she can do to encourage more people to attend her events.

Step Two: Knowledge

What does she need to know in order to figure out what to do? A couple of potential factors are timing (time of year, day of the week, time of the events), content (types of wines being reviewed), or experience (could be a wide variety of reasons, from the person presenting to the availability of parking for the events).

Step Three: Data

What needs to be measured? How many events people have attended, what motivated them to attend in the past, whether they attending more this year than last, what factors into their decision about whether to attend, and what their experience was at the last event they attended.

Step Four: Questions

This step focuses on crafting a series of great questions that not only get at each of the data elements but also provides you with actionable feedback. From step two above, we know there are three factors that we believe may be impacting attendance at our events. Each of these factors needs to be connected to the individual's perception of whether he or she has attended more or fewer events in the last six months than they may have attended prior to this period of time. Therefore, the questions that we want to answer are the following:

1. Event Attendance History:
   Q. How many events have you attended in the last six months?

   Q. Would you say that your attendance to our events has increased, decreased, or stayed relatively the same in the past six months compared to prior years?

2. Rationale for Change:
   Q. If you have either increased or decreased your attendance rate, please indicate below by ranking the following topics from highest to lowest, what influenced your decision to change your attendance.

A. Timing of events (day of the week, time of events, etc.)

B. Content (the types of wines being covered)

C. Experience (presenter, setting, parking)

3. Details:
   Q. Please provide us with further information on the item that you ranked highest in influencing your attendance to our events.

FORMULATE YOUR QUESTIONS

The questions outlined above take into account a number of the best practices for creating questions. Here are the five keys to successful question writing.

1. **Keep it short.** You are asking your participants to spend their time helping you out. You owe it to them to keep your survey short and to the point. If possible, keep the number of questions to ten or less.

2. **Start smart.** Start with the most important questions first and make them easy to answer so that your participant gets engaged in the process. If the first questions ask too much of the person taking the survey, he or she will just stop taking it, and you won't get any feedback.

3. **Know when to use closed- versus open-ended questions.** Closed-ended questions are sometimes also called quantitative questions. The benefits of these questions are that they are typically easier to respond to. Since you specify the potential answer set, they are also very easy to analyze. The challenges involved with these type of questions are that the provided answer set needs to be comprehensive and you need to know exactly what you want. An example of a closed-ended question is the following:
   Q. In comparing the past six months to the prior six months, would you say that your attendance at our events has increased, decreased, or stayed roughly the same?

An open-ended question is often called a qualitative question. The benefits of these questions are that the participant is not limited to your choices, and you are able to get results in the actual words of the participant. The challenges of these questions are that they cause fatigue on the participant (since they are harder to complete), you tend to get more feedback from the people on the extremes (really like or dislike), and the data is more difficult to analyze. An example of an open-ended question is the following:

Q. Please provide us with further information on the item that you ranked highest in influencing your attendance at our events.

4. **Right order gets results.** The order of your questions matters. Put the most important questions you want answered at the front of the survey. That way if the participant tires and does not finish the survey, you still have the answers to the most important questions. To make it easier on your readers, try to start your survey with closed-ended questions and place the open-ended questions and any demographic questions toward the end.

5. **Do something.** The first thing to do when someone has taken your survey is to thank him or her for taking the time. The next thing is to take action on the feedback he or she has provided and let the respondent know that the feedback factored into your actions. In our example above, the wine store owner, once learning that the biggest reason people stopped coming to her wine tasting events was a lack of available parking, should announce to her customers that she appreciated their feedback and that she has arranged free parking with the bank across the street from her store.

BE A DRIP

I suggest using a "drip" strategy, where you constantly collect small amounts of information rather than trying to do it all at once through one giant survey. You are more likely to benefit by getting real-time actionable content if you collect information on an ongoing basis. By using just one closed-ended question in conjunction with one open-ended question, you can get specific feedback on what you need to know and provide your customers with an opportunity to share with you what's on their mind.

Four Key Places to Collect Feedback

Not surprisingly, the four key places to collect feedback coincide with points throughout the Constant Contact Cycle I showed you in Chapter 2. Outlined below are the most important places you should be collecting feedback. I also show you the types of feedback you should be looking for in each place.

COLLECTING FEEDBACK ON YOUR WEB SITE

You can make your web site a lot more engaging and interactive by simply adding an online poll to your home page and using your emails to invite people to visit the page. A poll is nothing more than a one-question anonymous survey where the question and the possible answers to the question are displayed on your web site.

Since the question and answers are displayed, the visitor is afforded a risk-free way to check out your personality and test out the waters on the value that making a connection with your business can provide. Not unlike the content you are creating for your email communications, it is important when creating poll questions to keep them short, engaging, and closely tied to the products or services for which you are an expert.

WELCOMING FEEDBACK WITH YOUR WELCOME EMAIL

When someone first joins your email list and receives your welcome email, this initial connection is a great point to learn more about your new subscriber's interests and how he or she found you. Using your welcome email to link to a short two-question survey is sufficient to provide you with great actionable information without overwhelming a new member to your community.

ASKING IN YOUR EMAIL COMMUNICATIONS

Every communication you send should include at least one link that provides you with feedback from your readers. In addition to using feedback to help you write content as we outlined above, I believe all communications should also include a link to a series of one-question surveys that help you keep a finger on the pulse of your customers.

By creating a series of four key questions that you rotate through your email communications, you will be able to not only judge the current pulse of your customers, but you will also be able to track changes over time. The four key pieces of information every business should know:

1. Your customers' perception of the products/services you provide.

2. Your customers' perception of your approachability.

3. Your customers' propensity to tell others about you.

4. What you can do to provide even better service.

FEEDBACK FROM POST-PURCHASE FOLLOW-UP

The best time to get feedback on a customer's experience is immediately after he or she has interacted with you. As time passes, our memories of our experiences start to deteriorate. Eventually, only those people who had an extraordinarily positive or negative experience will remember anything about the interaction. Therefore, strike while the iron is hot and ask your recent customers for feedback on their experience while it is still fresh in their minds. Invite them to take a survey by adding recent shoppers to a separate email list and emailing them an invitation to take your post-purchase survey.

14

Getting Beyond the Inbox

The return on the investment you make in writing great email marketing content does not have to end when your email hits your recipients' inbox. In fact, you can keep this content alive and working on your behalf well into the future if you create an archive of your content. An archive is nothing more than an online library of your content linked together by an index of all of your campaigns. The great thing about creating an online library is that you can direct prospective customers there to actually see the value you provide to your readers as an additional motivator for getting them to join your list. Provided your archive is set up correctly, it can also be indexed by search engines like Google. By archiving each campaign you can use the articles you have created to attract new potential customers, and demonstrate to interested potential readers the value that you deliver to people on your list. It enables your content can stay alive forever and become a go-to resource for customers and prospects alike.

This chapter covers how to create and manage an email archive and how to maximize its impact.

Creating and Managing an Email Archive

An email archive is comprised of two different elements that both work together:

1. **An archive home page.** A central web page that contains information about your business and links to each of your archived emails (see Figure 14.1).

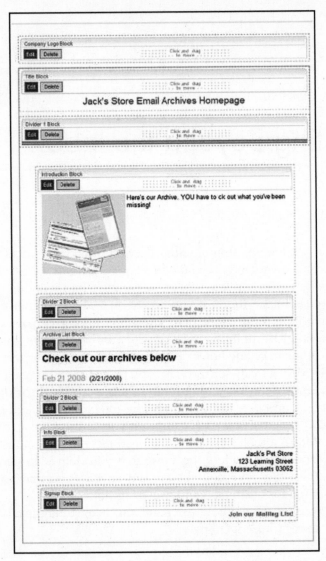

Figure 14.1   An archive home page template allows you to create a page listing your archived emails.

2. **Archived email pages.** Each email is turned into its own distinct web page.

The following sections describe how to set up and use each of these elements and explain additional features your archive should have.

SETTING UP AN ARCHIVE HOME PAGE

If you have the ability to update your own web site, you can create your own archive page by simply adding another page to your web site. If you don't have the ability to update your own web site, you can hire a web designer to set one up for you, or you can use the archive home page feature provided by your Email Service Provider. (See Figure 14.2.)

Whether you use your own web page or the one provided to you through a service, set up your archive home page with the following features.

♦ Include your logo at the top of the archive page and use the same color scheme as your web site.

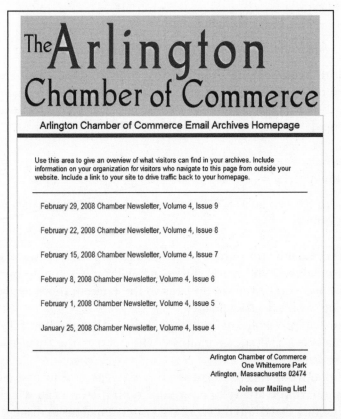

Figure 14.2   Some ESPs provide easy-to-use email archive features.

♦ Use the opening paragraph on the page to describe the value of the archive and give your visitors instructions.

♦ Use your search keywords in the content on your page so search engines can index and rank your email archive.

♦ Designate a prominent area of the page to list the links to your archived emails. (I'll show you how to create that in a bit.)

♦ Include a sign-up link on the archive home page so visitors can join your email list. That way, they won't have to visit the archive to receive new information.

In addition to these basic elements, your archive home page can also be customized to include background information on your business, contact information on how to reach you, and links to a poll or online survey.

ADDING ARCHIVED EMAILS TO YOUR ARCHIVE HOME PAGE

After you create a home page to host links to your email archives, you'll need to archive your emails and post links to them on your archive home page. Two easy ways to archive your emails are the following:

♦ Save your email as a PDF and post a link to it so people can download it.

♦ Save your email as HTML and post a link to it so people can read it online.

I recommend you archive your emails as HTML, because the links in your email will still work, the emails will be searchable by search engines, and you can make updates to the content more easily since the emails won't be downloaded.

Your ESP probably has an archive feature that automatically saves your emails as HTML and generates a unique link to the email as shown in Figure 14.3.

Think of your email archive as a catalog of all of your past information. You have the ability to customize both the order in which your campaigns are listed and the names of your campaigns to make it easier for your content to be found within the index.

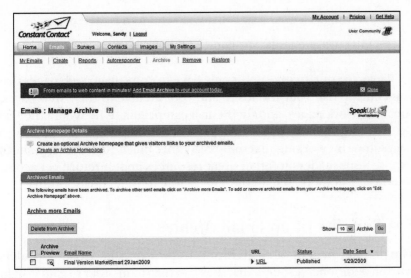

Figure 14.3   ESPs allow you to save your emails as HTML archives.

You can archive any email campaign you send and add it to your archive home page. Here are a few of the emails you should consider archiving on a regular basis:

♦ Newsletters

♦ Promotions that never expire

♦ Press releases

♦ Company announcements

Links to your archived emails don't have to live alone on your archive home page. You can also link to individual archived emails or your archive home page on other web sites. Some logical places under your own control where you should embed a link to your archived emails include

♦ Your web site home page.

♦ Next to your sign-up page for your email list.

♦ On every communication you send to your list.

♦ On your welcome letter that you send to new recipients.

♦ On your Facebook, MySpace, LinkedIn pages.

Links to your archive don't only have to come from web pages that you control. Ask your friends to add your archive to their web pages, social network pages, and their email campaigns. Why would they do that? Because you can put links to their email archives on your web pages, too. By working together with other business owners, you can expose your readers to other great resources and in return get access to other customers. It's simply a great way to build relationships!

The Benefits of an Email Archive

The primary benefit of an archive is to provide your existing readers with an additional resource that they can turn to in order to gain insight from you as an expert on an ongoing basis. However, there are a lot of other additional benefits as described in the following sections.

ATTRACTING NEW CUSTOMERS

Once your archive pages are published, search engines such as Google will be able to crawl your email content and add it to their search indexes. This means that as individuals search on Google and other search engines, your content may become one of the search results that are displayed. If you are interested in maximizing the potential of your email content showing up as a search result, you should contact a search engine specialist who can help you optimize your archive pages by the inclusion of meta tags and links from your web site as well as others to your archive page.

The fact that individuals can find your email content from search results makes it important to include a link to join your mailing list not only on the home page but on each campaign as well. By doing so, if a visitor finds your content appealing, you are well positioned to convince them to join your mailing list.

DEMONSTRATING VALUE

One of the challenges with web sites is that you are not there in person to meet and greet your visitors. By prominently positioning a link to your archive on your web site home page, you can provide web site visitors with a means through which to get to know you. Putting the link close to your "Join my mailing list" link on your web site will also give those individuals interested in your email list the ability to see what you are going to be sending. Setting a recipient's expectations for the quality of what he or she will be receiving when signing up for your communications will greatly improve the likelihood that he or she will open your campaign when it arrives.

For example, Rothman's, a men's clothing store in New York City, puts out a copy of one of their campaigns in a laminate frame by each of their cash registers. It provides patrons with something to look at while the employee is ringing up their purchases and draws their attention to the sign-up form just in front of the frame. This is another example of how setting expectations can not only add to your sign-ups but also maximize the impact of each campaign sent.

PROVIDING EXISTING READERS WITH A DESTINATION

Since your archive has the potential to bring all of your past email campaigns to life, it is a great resource for your existing customers to bookmark and return to whenever they have a question that has to do with your area of expertise. In addition, it provides new recipients with the ability to gain access to your past knowledge. Therefore, always include a link to your archive on every email campaign you send out. You can also feature a snippet from a past campaign and link to this specific article in order to keep the old content circulating through for your newer audience.

I am often asked about whether a small business or organization should have a blog. The answer is that it depends on the business you are in. However, if you are like most of the business owners that I know, your time is very limited and the challenge of writing a daily or bi-daily blog seems daunting. By creating an archive of your email content, you are essentially creating a blog of your ideas and insights. While it may not be as sexy as the daily reporting on Techcrunch or Coyoteblog, it's a lot more manageable.

CREATING EMAIL LANDING PAGES

If your website is more of an online brochure that stays static, you can use archived emails as web pages for the promotions featured in your emails.

You can also create two versions of your email campaign to keep your content more concise. To do this, create one version that is short and includes only the introductory paragraph of your content and the other that includes the entire article. Then post the long version to your archive and use the link provided for each archive page as the link in the short version that you send out to your recipients. This enables you to not only keep your email campaigns short but also provides an easy way to store the full content without having to have someone create an entirely new web page on your web site.

About the Author

Eric Groves has more than 20 years of experience helping companies of all sizes build sales, attract new business, and create online marketing strategies, but he takes particular pride in working with small business owners to help them channel their passion and realize success. Eric was the executive director of worldwide sales and business development at AltaVista. He also held leadership positions at iAtlas Corp., InfoUSA, Inc., MFS Communications, SBC Communications (now AT&T), and Citicorp. Eric served on the Board of Directors of LogoWorks (acquired by Hewlett Packard) and is currently on the board at Hubcast.

A sought-after speaker, Eric has shared his insights with thousands of attendees on behalf of the Small Business Administration, U.S. Chamber of Commerce, Association of Small Business Development Centers, and many other industry organizations. He has also been interviewed for *The Boston Globe*, *Entrepreneur*, *BusinessWeek*, *Fortune*, *BtoB*, and *Business Strata*.

At Constant Contact, which he joined in January 2001, Eric serves as senior vice president of global market development. In this capacity, he built the sales and business development departments from the ground up, including the creation of a network of regional development directors around the country. Eric was also instrumental in the expansion of the company's educational and content resources, which were the foundation for this book. His work has propelled Constant Contact's growth to more than 300,000 customers. In addition, Eric created Constant Contact's charitable program, Cares4Kids (www.cares4kids.com), which allows customers to donate a free account to the nonprofit organization of their choice.

Eric holds a Bachelor of Arts degree from Grinnell College and a Master of Business Administration from the University of Iowa.

About Constant Contact

Since 1998, Constant Contact has been helping small businesses, associations, and nonprofits connect with their customers, clients, and members by delivering professional, easy-to-use services and coaching at a reasonable cost. Constant Contact champions the needs of these organizations and allows them to create professional-looking email newsletters and insightful online surveys that help build successful, lasting relationships with their customers. Today, more than 300,000 customers worldwide trust Constant Contact to help them connect with their audiences.

Index